# SPAIN

## MEDITERRANEAN CUISINE

# SPAIN

## MEDITERRANEAN CUISINE

KÖNEMANN

# Contents

# List of Recipes

**Difficulty:**

★         easy
★★       medium
★★★     difficult

### Tapas  8

### Hot & Cold Appetizers  28

### Soups  62

## Fish & Seafood  82

## Meat & Poultry  126

## Desserts & Pastries  154

Tapas

# Basque

Preparation time: 45 minutes
Cooking time: 15 minutes
Level of difficulty: ★

**Serves 4**

4 cups/1 l    olive oil

**For the gilda:**
4    guindillas (hot green chiles) in vinegar
8    anchovy fillets in oil
8    green olives

**For the hake txorradita:**
2¼ lb/1 kg    hake
2    egg yolks

4 tsp/20 g    flour
1    red bell pepper
1 clove    garlic
    salt and pepper

**For serving:**
4 slices    country bread

**For the breaded anchovies with green chiles:**
4    fresh anchovies
4    green chiles (pimientos de Guernica)
1    egg yolk
4 tsp/20 g    flour
    salt

**For the garnish:**
    cherry tomatoes
    green bell pepper
    ground paprika (to taste)
    a little olive oil

As everywhere in Spain, the culinary traditions handed down in the Basque country are firmly anchored in the past. Every "bodega" has its own recipes for tapas, known as *pintxos* in Basque. Tapas are much more than snacks intended to stimulate the appetite; these little meals are an essential part of Iberian cuisine.

Enjoying a selection of *pintxos* with a glass of wine (*txikiteo*) is something of a ritual. In the Basque country, as elsewhere in Spain, the focus is on conviviality. Emilio Gonzalez Soto suggests three typical Basque recipes that illustrate the abundance of this unique cuisine.

The most popular dish in the *Pais Vasco* is fish, especially anchovies, in lots of variations. Every year at the beginning of fall, shoals of these tiny fish cross the Gulf of Biscay heading for Norway. The anchovy fillets that are processed in the canneries along the Cantabrian coast are widely regarded as the best on the Iberian Peninsula.

Anchovies prepared traditionally as *anchoada* are the most popular. To make this specialty, the cleaned fish—heads removed—are packed in wooden barrels, then marinated in brine. They are rinsed off after six months, filleted by hand, then packed in cans in olive or sunflower oil.

The two anchovy recipes provided by our chefs are easy to reproduce, and wonderfully spicy. Gilda is made with *guindillas*—very spicy green chiles that are pickled in vinegar. If you prefer something less fiery, choose a different variety. Green chile peppers from Guernica, for instance, are milder.

*To make the gilda, pierce one chile with a cocktail stick, then add an anchovy fillet and an olive to each side.*

*For the hake txorradita, remove the head and tail of the hake. Separate the fillets, then cut into pieces of equal sizes. Fry the bread in olive oil, then set aside.*

*Beat the egg yolks in a bowl. Season the fish with salt and pepper, then dip in the flour and coat with the beaten egg. Fry in the olive oil.*

# Pintxos

Roast the red bell pepper in an oven for about 15 minutes, then skin and cut into slices. Fry the slices in olive oil, then sprinkle over the chopped garlic.

For the breaded anchovies with green chile, beat the egg yolk in a bowl. Season the anchovies with salt, then turn in the flour and coat with beaten egg.

Fry the anchovy fillets and green chile together in olive oil. Arrange the pintxos on a plate. Serve with halved cherry tomatoes and bell pepper rings, a little olive oil, ground paprika, and the fried bread.

# Tapas

Preparation time:   30 minutes
Cooking time:       15 minutes
Difficulty:         ★

**Serves 4**

**For the fritura andaluza:**

| | |
|---|---|
| 2 cups/500 g | chanquetes or fresh anchovies |
| 7/8 cup/100 g | flour |
| 2 cups/500 ml | olive oil |
| | lemon |
| | salt |

**For the gambas:**

| | |
|---|---|
| 2 cups/500 g | gambas |
| 1 | dried chile pod |

| | |
|---|---|
| 1 clove | garlic |
| 7 tbsp/100 ml | olive oil |
| 5 | parsley stalks |
| 1 | small glass white wine |
| | salt |

**For the toast with chorizo:**

| | |
|---|---|
| 4 slices | baguette |
| 1 clove | garlic |
| 1 | ripe tomato |
| 1 | small, mild chorizo sausage |
| 4 slices | pork loin, marinated a little native olive oil |

The Spanish like to meet up with friends in a café before lunch for a drink and a few little appetizers, called tapas. José-Ignacio Herráiz recommends—in addition to the extremely popular tiny deep-fried anchovies and spicy pork loin with chorizo—tapas "the Granada way."

*Chanquetes* are tiny young fish that are not usually found anywhere outside Andalusia. You can also use anchovies, small sardines, red snapper, or slices of stockfish (dried salted cod). The chef uses extra-fine wheat meal for the coating, which adheres to the fish in a thin layer, retaining its moisture and aroma. If you only have ordinary household flour to hand, shake off any excess flour in a sieve. Deep-fry small portions of the fish in very hot oil.

*Gambas de huelva* are the most popular of all Spanish shrimp varieties. Many Spaniards even suck out the heads—although maybe not necessarily in a smart restaurant. To accommodate these connoisseurs, José-Ignacio Herráiz has come up with something really special: he fries the heads in oil, then pushes them through a sieve. He collects the aromatic juices and serves them with the gambas. Incidentally, scampi can also be used for this recipe.

Ready-marinated pork loin is available all over Spain, but it is not difficult to do it yourself at home. Bring the water to the boil with some thyme, oregano, garlic, cloves, and cinnamon, then leave to cool. Cut the pork loin into slices, marinate in the water together with some ground paprika, and leave for two days. If you do not have any chorizo, you can also use a mixture of ground meat, garlic, parsley, and ground paprika as a filling.

*Salt the fish for the fritura andaluza. Sprinkle the flour on a plate, and coat the fish in it, using your fingers to turn them. Place in a sieve and shake to remove the excess.*

*Heat the oil in a pot until very hot, then deep-fry the fish until light yellow. Remove with a spatula and place on paper towels. Arrange on a plate garnished with lemon slices.*

*Peel the gambas and cut them open to remove the innards. Crumble the dried chile. Slice the garlic, fry in the oil, then add the chile.*

# from Andalusia

Salt the gambas and fry in the spiced oil, making sure it is very hot. Sprinkle with chopped parsley and cook for 1 minute, then pour over the white wine and continue cooking.

Toast the bread slices. Peel the garlic. Halve the tomatoes. As soon as the bread is crunchy, rub the surface with the garlic and tomato. Remove the outer skin from the chorizo and dry fry the sausage; reduce the juices a little.

Beat the pork loins until flat, then fry on each side in a skillet with a little oil and garlic for 30 seconds. Place a little chorizo on each side, fold over the other end and secure with a cocktail stick. Repeat with the remaining slices of bread.

# Tapas

Preparation time: 1 hour
Cooking time: 30 minutes
Difficulty: ★

**Serves 4**

| | |
|---|---|
| 2 cups/500 ml | olive oil for deep frying |

**For the palillos:**

| | |
|---|---|
| 1 oz/25 g | smoked bacon |
| 1 | mushroom |
| ½ | onion |
| ⅛ stick/15g | butter |
| 1 tsp/5 g | flour |
| 7 tbsp/100 ml | milk |
| 2 tbsp/30 ml | brandy |
| 4 | dates |
| 2 slices | bacon |
| | salt and pepper |

**For the bread and ham:**

| | |
|---|---|
| 1 oz/25 g | ham |
| 2 oz/50 g | cepes |

| | |
|---|---|
| 2 oz/50 g | green beans |
| 2 oz/50 g | green asparagus |
| 1 tsp/5 g | baking soda |
| 1 tsp/5 g | butter |
| 2 tsp/10 g | Roquefort |
| 4 slices | white bread |
| | a little olive oil |

**For the stuffed eggplants:**

| | |
|---|---|
| 2 oz/50 g | mushrooms |
| 1 | onion |
| 4 oz/100 g | ground meat |
| | a little olive oil |
| 2 tbsp/30 ml | brandy |
| 2 tbsp/30 ml | milk |
| 2 tsp/10 g | flour |
| 4 | eggplants |
| 3½ tbsp/50 g | grated cheese |
| | salt |

**For the Spanish sauce:**

| | |
|---|---|
| 4 tbsp/60 ml | olive oil |
| ½ | diced onion |
| ½ | finely chopped carrot |
| 1 | leek |
| 1 | tomato |
| 1 glass | port |
| 1 tbsp/15 g | flour |
| 2 tbsp | tomato concentrate |
| 2 tsp | sugar |
| | salt and pepper |

The best way to get to know the cuisine of any Spanish region is to start with the tapas, which are served in almost every bar. They are the expression of the typically Spanish *joie de vivre*. This also applies to Alicante. Vast selections of tasty tapas are popular all over this holiday resort on the Costa Blanca. *Palillos*, literally "toothpicks," are ideal with an aperitif. These spicy filled dates, wrapped in bacon, are a salty-sweet culinary treat. The fruit is characteristic of the Alicante region. The first date palms were introduced by the Carthaginians. The Arabs continued with the cultivation, and built up their own date plantations. In the 12th century the town of Elche had a date grove that today boasts nearly 400,000 palms, making it one of the biggest in Europe.

*Platos gratinados*, or gratins are a specialty of Alicante. The eggplants in this recipe, filled with meat and mushrooms, seasoned with garlic, then baked with cheese, are a delicacy. To make the Spanish sauce, heat the olive oil in a pot and sauté first the diced onion, finely chopped carrot, leek, and tomato. Pour over half the port, and leave the vegetables to simmer for 5 minutes. Then season to taste with salt and pepper. Add the flour and tomato concentrate, pour over a little water, and simmer for an hour. In a second pot, caramelize the sugar until light brown, then remove from the heat and pour over the remaining port. Simmer gently for one minute, and then add it to the sauce.

*For the palillos, finely chop the smoked bacon, mushroom, and onion, and sauté in the butter. Season with salt. Add the flour and milk, and simmer gently for 2 minutes, then pour over the brandy and season with pepper.*

*Pit the dates, fill with the mixture, and wrap each one in a strip of bacon. Secure with a cocktail stick, and fry in olive oil.*

*For the bread and ham, chop the ham, cepes, beans, and asparagus very finely. Blanch the beans and asparagus separately in water with a little baking soda. Fry the ham in the butter, add the chopped vegetables, then season with salt and sauté for 3 minutes.*

# from Alicante

Add the Roquefort, and simmer for 1 further minute. Fry the bread slices in olive oil, and spread liberally with this mixture.

For the eggplant stuffing, finely chop the mushrooms and onion, and combine with the ground meat. Fry the mixture in olive oil, season with salt, and pour over the brandy. Add the milk and flour, and stir well.

Prepare the Spanish sauce as described opposite. Scoop out the eggplants and bake in the oven (350 °F/180 °C). Fill with this mixture, sprinkle over the cheese, and return to the oven for 5 minutes. Arrange the tapas on plates.

# Tapas

Preparation time: 1 hour
Soaking the
   stockfish: 24 hours
Cooking time: 1 hour 30 minutes
Difficulty: ★

**Serves 4**

**For the tomato bread:**
| | |
|---|---|
| 1 | eggplant |
| 1 | red bell pepper |
| | a little olive oil |
| 4 slices | white bread |
| 2 | ripe tomatoes |
| 4 | anchovy fillets in brine |
| | salt |

**For the mushrooms with Spanish sausage:**
| | |
|---|---|
| 4 | milkcaps or chanterelles |

| | |
|---|---|
| 4 slices | blood sausage (Butifarra negra) |
| | a little olive oil |
| 2 cloves | garlic |
| 1 bunch | flat-leaf parsley |
| | salt and pepper |

**For the toast with diced stockfish:**
| | |
|---|---|
| 4 slices | white bread |
| 1 | large ripe tomato |
| ¾ cup/200 g | stockfish |
| scant 1 oz/20 g | black olives |
| | a little olive oil |
| ⅜ cup/50 g | flour |

*Pa amb tomàquet*—tomato toast—kindles childhood memories for many Catalans, but adults love toasted farmhouse bread rubbed with tomato and a dash of olive oil just as much.

For these tapas, our chef chose dark red, ripe tomatoes with plenty of juice and flavor. The bread is spread with *escalivada*. To make the *escalivada*, roast the bell pepper and eggplant in a hot oven or in a skillet so the flavor develops fully and the skins can be easily removed once cool. The eggplant will take much longer than the bell pepper, which will be ready after about 30 minutes; the eggplant will take about another 30 to 40 minutes. After rubbing them with tomato and spreading them with *escalivada*, the slices of bread are topped with anchovy fillets; Pep Masiques believes that the anchovies from the village of L'Escala near Gerona are the best.

The second tapas variety reveals the Catalans' passion for forest mushrooms and sausage. *Butifarra negra* is a specialty of Catalonia. It is finer and drier than most types of blood sausage, and is made of pig's blood, lean meat, and spices. It is cut into slices, which are fried for just a few moments. The mushrooms take a little longer. Milkcaps are particularly popular. However, if you are unable to find them, chanterelles are an excellent substitute.

The chef's third choice of tapas is an original delicious combination of stockfish (dried salted cod), black olives, and olive oil. The bread for this dish is cut more thinly than for the tomato bread.

The stockfish must be soaked in water for one or two days beforehand. You can speed up the process by holding it under running water for a while.

*For the tomato bread, wash and dry the eggplant and bell pepper. Place on an oiled baking sheet and drizzle over some oil. Bake in the oven (430 °F/220 °C) for 1 hour. Rinse under cold water, then remove the skin and cut the vegetables into slices. Toast the bread in the oven.*

*Rub each slice of bread with half a tomato, drizzle over some olive oil, and sprinkle with salt. Place 3 strips each of bell pepper and eggplant on top, and arrange with the anchovy fillets.*

*Wipe the mushrooms with a cloth and remove the stalks. Fry the heads and the blood sausage in a little hot oil, then season with salt and pepper.*

# from Catalonia

Alternate the mushrooms and blood sausage on cocktail sticks. Peel the garlic, chop finely with the parsley and combine with olive oil. Garnish the skewers with this sauce.

For the stockfish toast, toast the bread in the oven until golden. Skin the tomatoes, remove the seeds, and cut into quarters. Dice the soaked stockfish, and remove the skin and bones. Pit the olives and chop them finely, then mash to a paste with a little olive oil.

Coat the fish pieces in flour and fry in oil. Arrange a tomato quarter and a piece of fish on each slice of bread, and drizzle with the olive sauce.

# Tapas

| | |
|---|---|
| Preparation time: | *1 hour* |
| Marinating time: | *5 hours* |
| Cooking time: | *40 minutes* |
| Difficulty: | ★★★ |

**Serves 4**

**For the marinade**

| | |
|---|---|
| 4 tbsp/60 ml | olive oil |
| | vinegar |
| 2 tsp | oregano |
| 1 tsp | cumin |
| | salt and pepper |

**For the lamb tripe:**

| | |
|---|---|
| 2 | lamb's tripe |
| 4 | vine tendrils |
| | a little olive oil for frying |
| 1 lb 2 oz/500 g | wholegrain bread |

**For the almagro eggplant:**

| | |
|---|---|
| ²/₃ cup/150 ml | water |
| ²/₃ cup/150 ml | sherry vinegar |
| 1 | red bell pepper |
| 1 | dried chile pod (guindilla) |

| | |
|---|---|
| 2 tsp | cumin |
| 2 tsp | ground paprika (pimiento) |
| 2 tbsp | dried oregano |
| 4 | dwarf eggplants |
| 4 tbsp/60 ml | olive oil |
| | salt and pepper |

**For the quail in honey sauce:**

| | |
|---|---|
| 2 | quail |
| 5 tsp/25 g | honey |
| 7 tbsp/100 ml | sherry vinegar |
| 1 sprig | rosemary |
| 2 tbsp/30 g each | bacon and Serrano ham |
| 1 | leek (white part) |
| | oil for deep frying |
| | salt and pepper |

When enjoying the delights of the tapas from the region of La Mancha, it is easy to picture Don Quixote and his faithful Sancho Panza philosophizing over a pitcher of wine and delicacies such as these tapas.

The specialty of Cuerca, the chef's native village, is lamb's tripe. This rustic dish is very popular, and is usually eaten sprinkled with lemon juice. Marinating it for five hours makes the tripe wonderfully aromatic. Make sure the tripe you buy is clean and white, and do not forget to wrap it in vine tendrils.

Like Don Quixote and his manservant, we too are embarking on a culinary voyage to Almagro in the south of La Mancha. The town is as famous for its theatrical festival as it is for its eggplants. Every year, it produces some 5,000 tons of this fabulous vegetable.

The small oval *berenjenas de Almagro* (Almagro eggplants) are prized all over the Iberian peninsula. They are harvested from July to September, after which they are cooked and then preserved. This form of preparation is also recommended by Alberto Herráiz. The reputation of *orza*, eggplant cooked traditionally in a small ceramic pot, extends far beyond La Mancha. They are available as preserves in good delicatessens.

Quail are also an essential part of typical Catalan tapas. They are served with a sweet sauce that typifies the finesse and wealth of the region's cuisine.

*For the tripe, stir together 4 tbsp of olive oil, vinegar, oregano, and cumin for the marinade. Season with salt and pepper. Marinate the tripe in this mixture for five hours. Then wrap the tripe in vine tendrils and boil in water for about 15 minutes.*

*Cut the cooked tripe into slices and fry in the remainder of the oil. Meanwhile, toast the bread in the oven.*

*For the eggplants, mix together the water and sherry vinegar. Cut the bell pepper into strips, and add with the chile and 1 tsp each of cumin, ground paprika, and oregano. Bring to the boil and add the eggplants. Cook for 10–15 minutes.*

# "Don Quixote"

Skewer the eggplants onto little sticks. Garnish with strips of bell pepper. Make a sauce of olive oil, the remaining cumin, ground paprika, and oregano. Season with salt and pepper.

Joint the quail and remove the legs; season with salt and pepper. For the sauce, put the honey, vinegar, and rosemary in a pot and boil briefly; season with salt.

Wrap the quail drumsticks in bacon and ham. Bake in the oven (400 °F/200 °C) for 10–12 minutes. For the garnish, cut the leek into fine strips and deep-fry. Arrange the tapas on plates and serve.

# Tapas

Preparation time: 1 hour
Resting time for
the dough: 1 hour
Cooking time: 1 hour 5 minutes
Difficulty: ★★

**Serves 4**

**For the empanadillas:**

| | |
|---|---|
| ⁷/₈ cup/100 g | flour |
| 1 packet | dried yeast |
| 5 tsp/25 g | shortening |
| 4 tbsp/60 ml | milk |
| 6½ tbsp/100 ml | olive oil |
| | salt |

**For the filling:**

| | |
|---|---|
| 1 each | onion, green bell pepper, red bell pepper, zucchini, tomato |
| 4 oz/100 g | tuna |

| | |
|---|---|
| 1 sprig | oregano |
| | oil for deep frying |
| | salt and pepper |

**For the almond mangold:**

| | |
|---|---|
| 4 oz/100 g | ham |
| 2 cups/500 g | mangold |

| | |
|---|---|
| 2 | eggs |
| 1 clove | garlic |
| 1¼ cups/150 g | flour |
| 1 packet | dried yeast |
| 1¼ cups/300 ml | carbonated mineral water |
| | pinch of sugar |
| 7 tbsp/100 g | flaked almonds |
| | olive oil for deep frying |
| | salt and pepper |

**For the summer salad:**

| | |
|---|---|
| 2 | medium potatoes |
| 8 tbsp/120 ml | olive oil |
| 3 tbsp/45 ml | sherry vinegar |
| 1 | scallion (spring onion) |
| 4–5 | parsley stalks |
| 2 | eggs |
| 1 | red bell pepper |
| 8 | anchovy fillets |
| 4 slices | bread to serve |
| | salt and pepper |

Whether in a small village or the smart urban area of a city, tapas bars are popular meeting places. The best bars serve a range of between two and three dozen delights to enjoy with an aperitif.

*Empanadillas*—stuffed pastry pockets—are typical of Madrid. The other two recipes are creations by Julio Reoyo. He garnishes the summer salad with *piquillos*, mild bell peppers that are broiled and preserved in oil.

Traditionally, mangold is cut into pieces, blanched, coated, and deep-fried. The chef finishes them off with ham, egg, and flaked almonds. Remove the green from the mangold leaves, pull the threads away from the stalks, and cut the stalks into pieces.

Julio Reoyo uses country-cured ham, *jamón de jabugo*, for its aroma. The ham comes from black pigs that are fed on acorns in the woodlands of the Extremadura. The ingredients are all wrapped in a light-as-a-feather batter that owes its lightness to the combination of yeast and sparkling mineral water. Deep-frying them in hot oil seems to transform the packages into light, airy, melt-in-the-mouth beignets.

In marked contrast to this are *empanadillas*, which are filled with various vegetables and tuna (*atún*). The bell peppers are deseeded and then chopped into tiny pieces. The dough is rolled out and cut into shapes 3 in (8 cm) in diameter. The edges are brushed with olive oil and the circles folded in half over the filling.

*For the empanadillas, combine the flour with the yeast, shortening, salt, milk, and oil in a bowl. Knead until smooth. Leave to stand for 1 hour, then roll out and cut into circles.*

*Finely chop the onion, bell pepper, zucchini, tomato, and tuna. First fry the onion in hot oil, then the bell pepper, then sauté the bell pepper and zucchini. Add the tomato, tuna, oregano, salt, and pepper. Fill the dough circles with this mixture and deep-fry in hot oil.*

*Chop the ham for the mangold. Tear the mangold leaves into pieces and blanch. Boil the eggs for 10 minutes, then peel them and cut into slices. Cut the garlic into thin slices.*

# from Madrid

Thread the mangold, egg, ham, and garlic onto skewers. For the batter, whisk together the flour, yeast, salt, pepper, mineral water, and sugar. Dip the skewers in the batter and coat in the almonds. Deep-fry until golden.

For the summer salad, boil the potatoes in their skins, then peel and cut into thin slices. Whisk together the oil, vinegar, salt, pepper, the chopped green of a scallion, and chopped parsley, then coat the potato slices in it.

Boil the eggs for 10 minutes, then peel and cut into slices. Cut the bell pepper into thin slices. Arrange slices of potato and egg, strips of bell pepper, and anchovy fillets on the slices of bread.

# Tapas

*Preparation time:* 1 hour
*Cooking time:* 1 hour 30 minutes
*Difficulty:* ☆

**Serves 4**

**For the lentil crème:**

| | |
|---|---|
| 2 cups/500 g | green lentils |
| 1 | onion |
| 2 | potatoes |
| 1 | bay leaf |
| 2 | cloves |
| 1 | pork bone |
| 1 | veal bone |
| | salt |

**For the tomato jello:**

| | |
|---|---|
| 3 | ripe tomatoes |
| 2 sheets | gelatin |

splash of olive oil
salt

**For the clams with vegetable vinaigrette:**

| | |
|---|---|
| 1 | red bell pepper |
| 1 | yellow bell pepper |
| 1 | green bell pepper |
| 1 | sour gherkin (to taste) |
| 1 | onion |
| 3 tbsp/45 ml | olive oil |
| 2 tbsp/30 ml | apple vinegar |
| 16 | clams |
| | salt |

**For the bacon skewers with beets:**

| | |
|---|---|
| 10 oz/250 g | salted, soaked neck of pork |
| 2 cups/500 g | beet leaves |
| 2 cloves | garlic |
| 1 lb 2 oz/500 g | potatoes |
| ⅛ stick/15 g | butter |
| 1 | chorizo sausage |
| 1 tbsp/15 ml | olive oil |
| | salt |

The tapas served in Spanish bars are a cross-section of the repertoire of the region's cuisine, and offer an excellent insight into the variety of regional specialties. To the Spanish, they are small, perfectly composed meals rather than snacks for in-between: they are rooted deeply in Iberian culture, and are a testimony to the country's rich gastronomic heritage.

The chef's tapas recipes are a culinary voyage through Galicia. *Grelos*, the tender leaves from the top of turnips, are an essential ingredient in hearty winter dishes and are especially popular at carnival time. The best substitute for *grelos* outside Spain is beets. They are usually served with salted pork and chorizo. Slightly spicy beet leaves go extremely well with puréed potatoes. What makes this recipe so original is the layering of the two vegetables in a glass, and serving them with a skewer of meat and sausage. You can also use spinach or kale instead of *grelos*.

Lentil crème on tomato jello is a creation by María Lourdes Fernández-Estevez. The combination of hot and cold works well. The best lentils to use are puy lentils, which have a thin outer skin, firm flesh, and a delicate aroma.

Galicia is on the north-west Atlantic coast, so it is hardly surprising that every menu contains various seafoods. Clams are particularly popular, and are usually served only with a dash of lemon juice. In this recipe the chef serves them with a delicious Mediterranean vegetable vinaigrette.

*Fill a pot with cold water, then bring the lentils, chopped onion, potatoes, bay leaf, cloves, and the bones to the boil. Simmer for about 1 hour. Season with salt, then remove the bones and purée the stock.*

*Dip the tomatoes in boiling water, then remove the skins and purée the flesh. Soak the gelatin in cold water. Heat a little olive oil in a pot, and heat the puréed tomatoes. Add the gelatin and stir. Season with salt.*

*To make the vinaigrette, finely chop the bell peppers, gherkin, and onion, and combine in a bowl with the olive oil and vinegar. Season with salt.*

# from Galicia

Wash the clams. Bring a pot of water to the boil, and cook the clams for 2 minutes. Remove the top half of the shell.

Put the pork in a pot of water, cover with a lid, and cook for 1½ hours. In a second pot, bring some salted water to the boil and add the beet leaves. Blanch for 1 minute, then drain. Sauté the chopped garlic and the leaves in olive oil. Purée.

Dice the potatoes and boil in salted water. Purée, then heat again and gradually add the butter, stirring continuously. Cut the chorizo into slices and fry, then skewer with the sliced pork, alternating between the two.

# Tapas

| | |
|---|---|
| *Preparation time:* | *45 minutes* |
| *Marinating time:* | *1 hour* |
| *Soaking time:* | *overnight* |
| *Cooking time:* | *1 hour 15 minutes* |
| *Difficulty:* | ✶ |

**Serves 4**

**For the anchovies in sherry vinegar:**

| | |
|---|---|
| 6 | large fresh anchovies |
| 3 tbsp/45 ml | sherry vinegar |
| 3 tbsp/45 ml | water |
| 1 clove | garlic, chopped |
| 2 tbsp/30 ml | olive oil |
| 1 sprig | rosemary |
| | salt and pepper |

**For the bell pepper escalivada:**

| | |
|---|---|
| 2 | green bell peppers, halved |
| 2 | red bell peppers, halved |
| 4 | silver onions |
| 2 | tomatoes |

| | |
|---|---|
| 2 tbsp/30 ml | olive oil |
| | chives |
| | salt and pepper |

**For the garbanzo beans with ham:**

| | |
|---|---|
| 4 tsp/20 g | dried garbanzo beans (chickpeas) |
| 4 tsp/20 g | dried cannellini beans |
| 1 | red bell pepper |
| 1 | green bell pepper |
| 2 | silver onions |
| 1 | carrot |
| 3 | parsley stalks |
| 1 clove | garlic |
| | olive oil |
| 2 slices | Serrano ham |
| 2 slices | white bread |
| | salt and pepper |

Javier Valero suggests three classic yet very simple tapas. These tapas are typical of the region, and are served with aperitifs in Málaga's bars.

The anchovies are marinated in a spicy combination of olive oil, sherry vinegar, garlic, and rosemary. The marinating time depends on the size of the fish, but an hour is usually ideal. The color and aroma of the anchovies are enhanced by the addition of a pinch of ground paprika. The anchovies are garnished with aromatic rosemary leaves.

The salad of red and green bell peppers is a typically Spanish *escalivada*, which is to say the vegetables are roasted in the oven or under the broiler until they are almost black. Other suitable vegetables are silver onions, tomatoes, and eggplants. The skin is then lifted away with a sharp knife. The vegetables are arranged in a bowl, a little olive oil drizzled over the top, and a garnish of chives added.

The salad of garbanzo beans and Serrano ham is spicy, and the combination of flavors and textures make it a delicious treat. The aroma is further intensified if the pulses are cooked in chicken stock with a little thyme and bay leaf. Remember that dried garbanzo beans and cannellini beans are as hard as stone, and need to be soaked overnight in cold water. Garnished with blanched julienne vegetables, fried ham, and croutons, the only thing still missing is perhaps a little parsley. If you like, a touch of cinnamon will round off this salad perfectly.

Anyone who likes high-quality, aromatic olive oil will not be disappointed by these tapas!

*Wash the anchovies, clean inside and remove the bones. Combine the vinegar and water, and marinate the anchovies in this for about 1 hour.*

*To make the dressing, combine the chopped garlic with the olive oil, rosemary, salt, and pepper in a bowl. Cut the marinated anchovies in half, arrange on a plate, and pour over the dressing. Garnish with rosemary leaves.*

*To make the escalivada, cover a baking sheet with aluminum foil, and roast the halved bell peppers and whole onions for about 10 minutes. Then remove the skins.*

# from Málaga

Cut the broiled bell peppers into strips. Dip the tomatoes in boiling water, then into cold, and remove the skins. Arrange the red and green bell peppers on a plate, and season with salt and pepper. Garnish with sliced tomatoes, onions, olive oil, and chives.

Boil the soaked garbanzo beans and cannellini beans for about 1 hour. Roast the bell peppers, onions, and garlic. Blanch the carrot and cut into julienne strips. Combine everything with chopped parsley, oil, salt, and pepper.

Sauté the ham and diced bread in olive oil in a skillet. Arrange the salad on a plate with ham and bread. Garnish with a little parsley.

Preparation time: 1 hour
Drying time for
   the tomatoes: 3 hours
Chilling time: 6 hours
Baking time for bell
   pepper tartlets: 10 minutes
Standing time (dough): 2 hours
Baking time for potatoes: 50 minutes
Difficulty: ★★

**Serves 4**

**For the tomato terrine:**

| | |
|---|---|
| 2¼ lb/1 kg | tomatoes |
| 2–3 sprigs | thyme |
| 2 cloves | garlic |
| | a little olive oil |
| 4 | quail's eggs |
| generous | |
| ⅓ cup/100 g | anchovies |
| few | basil stalks |

| | |
|---|---|
| 4 slices | white bread |
| | salt and pepper |

**For the bell pepper tartlets:**

| | |
|---|---|
| 1⅛ cup/125 g | flour |
| 1⅛ cup/125 g | wholemeal flour |
| 6½ tbsp/100 ml | olive oil |

| | |
|---|---|
| 2¼ lb/1 kg | red bell peppers |
| ¼ cup/50 g | mullet roe |
| 1 clove | garlic |
| | black olives |
| | parsley |
| | salt and pepper |

**For the baked potatoes with mussels:**

| | |
|---|---|
| 24 | mussels |
| 2 | smooth, medium-sized potatoes |
| 2 tbsp/30 ml | olive oil |

**For the lemon mayonnaise:**

| | |
|---|---|
| 2 | eggs |
| 1 cup/250 ml | olive oil |
| 1 tbsp/15 ml | lemon juice |
| ½ clove | garlic |
| 4–5 | parsley stalks |
| | salt |

Tapas are easy to make, but use high-quality ingredients. Oscar Torrijos got his ideas for his selection from the tapas bars of his home town of Valencia. Bell peppers, mussels, tasty, pizza-like tartlets known as *cocas*, and dishes that combine anchovies with tomatoes are all popular in Valencia.

The tomatoes for the terrine have to be dried in the oven for a while. They are then layered, alternately, with raw tomatoes and anchovies in a terrine and a weight put on top. It takes six hours for the terrine to "set," after which you can remove it carefully from the mold. Toast the bread in the oven or in a skillet, and cut the terrine and the bread into pieces of the same size. Then place the terrine on top of the bread. Skewer the quail's eggs on little sticks and use as a garnish.

The second recipe is for tartlets with bell peppers and roe. *Cocas* are similar to Italian pizza, and have always been popular in Valencia. Oscar Torrijos garnishes them with fried parsley and slices of mullet roe. *Mojama*, a kind of dried tuna, is equally good for this.

The third variety of tapas consists of potatoes that are either baked in the oven, or deep-fried. They are garnished and then gratineed with *clochinas*, a type of clam.

*Wash the tomatoes for the terrine, then cut into quarters and remove the seeds. Place 1 lb 10 oz (700 g) of them on a baking sheet. Sprinkle over thyme, salt, pepper, and chopped garlic, and a little olive oil. Dry in the oven for 3 hours (160 °F/80 °C). Boil the quail's eggs.*

*Line a rectangular mold with plastic wrap. Arrange alternate layers of dried tomatoes, anchovies, and raw tomatoes inside. Season with salt, pepper, basil, and oil. Cover with plastic wrap. Place a weight on top and leave for 6 hours. Arrange on toasted bread.*

*To make the tartlets, combine the flour with 4 tbsp (60 ml) oil and salt in a bowl, then knead until smooth. Shape in a ball and refrigerate for 2 hours. Roll out the dough, cut out circles, and bake in the oven for 10 minutes (400 °F/200 °C).*

# from Valencia

Roast the bell peppers, then remove the skins and seeds. Cut the bell peppers and roe into thin strips and combine in a bowl with the chopped garlic, pepper, and oil. Place this mixture on top of the tartlets. Garnish with olives and parsley.

Cook the mussels until they open, then remove from the shells. Peel the potatoes and cut in half lengthwise. Scoop out the insides to make "ships." Place on an oiled baking sheet and bake in the oven for 35 minutes (400 °F/200 °C).

Combine the ingredients for the mayonnaise, and season with garlic and chopped parsley. Place the mussels inside the potatoes, then top with the mayonnaise. Place briefly under the broiler.

# Hot & Cold Appetizers

# Ajo

Preparation time: 40 minutes
Standing time for
  the dough: 2 hours
Cooking time: 3 hours 35 minutes
Difficulty: ★★

**Serves 4**

**For the tomato tartlet with pine nuts:**
*Dough*:

| | |
|---|---|
| 2 cups/250 g | flour |
| ²/₃ cup/160 ml | oil |
| 2 | egg yolks |
| 7 tbsp/100 ml | water |
| | salt |

*Topping*:

| | |
|---|---|
| 1½ lb/600 g | plum tomatoes |
| 2 tbsp/30 g | pine nuts |

| | |
|---|---|
| 1 bunch | thyme, chopped |
| 2 cloves | garlic, chopped |
| | a little olive oil |
| | salt and pepper |

**For the ajo arriero:**

| | |
|---|---|
| 1 lb 2 oz/500 g | potatoes |
| 10 oz/250 g | stockfish, soaked and desalted |
| 1–2 cloves | garlic |
| | a little olive oil |
| 2 tbsp/30 g | pine nuts |
| 4–5 | black olives |
| 2 | eggs |

There used to be numerous muleteers, or *arrieros*, on Spain's country roads, transporting essential foods such as stockfish. While the muleteers were traveling, they would often prepare simple dishes over an open fire. Garlic—*ajo* in Spanish—was an important seasoning as it was easy to keep, and stored well.

Today, both the Spanish and the Portuguese still eat lots of stockfish—that is to say, dried salted cod. This large fish is not caught in the area, but comes from colder waters. Once abundant around Newfoundland, it now comes mainly from Norway.

Ajo arriero is similar to *brandade de morue* (salt cod paste), which is popular in the south of France. However, the Spanish version contains more potato. To make the dish even more appetizing, Oscar Torrijos serves it with tartlets topped with tomatoes and pine nuts.

Traditionally, the stockfish and potatoes were just roughly mashed by hand to give the mixture "bite," but you can make life easier by putting it all in the blender. The oil is added gradually to make the mixture smooth. If it is too thick, add a little of the water that the fish was cooked in.

In this recipe the cook garnishes the dumplings with boiled egg yolks, but sometimes they are added directly to the fish-and-potato mixture. There are countless variations of this dish in the country's various regions.

The tomato tartlets are similar to pizza. In Valencia, these small tartlets of flour, egg, and oil are called *coca*, and are topped with bell peppers or tomatoes. The cooking time can be reduced considerably by using ready prepared dried tomatoes, although they are much more aromatic if you prepare them yourself.

*To make the tartlets, sift the flour into a bowl and make a well in the middle. Add the salt, oil, egg yolks, and water, and knead until smooth. Shape into a bowl, wrap in plastic wrap, and chill for 2 hours.*

*For the topping, pour boiling water over the tomatoes and skin them. Cut them into quarters and remove the seeds. Place on a baking sheet, sprinkle with salt, pepper, thyme, and chopped garlic, then drizzle over the oil. Dry in the oven (190 °F/80 °C) for 2–3 hours.*

*For the ajo arriero, cut the potatoes into quarters and boil for 20 minutes. Cook the chopped stockfish in water for 10 minutes. Peel the garlic. Drain the stockfish, then remove the skin and bones.*

# Arriero

Put the potatoes, stockfish, and garlic in a bowl, then mash well.

Add a little olive oil and stir until smooth. Set aside. Toast the pine nuts. Roll out the pastry for the tartlets and cut out circles; pierce with a fork. Place on a baking sheet lined with baking parchment.

Top the tartlets with tomatoes and pine nuts, and drizzle over a little olive oil. Bake for 15 minutes. Arrange slices of the tartlets and the purée on plates. Garnish some of the ajo arriero with chopped olives, some with chopped boiled egg yolk.

# Anchovies with

Preparation time: 10 minutes
Marinating time: 10 hours
Chilling time: 3 hours
Difficulty: ★★

**Serves 4**

**For the raspberry oil:**
6½ tbsp/100 g    raspberries
1¼ cups/300 ml  olive oil

**For the anchovies:**
2 cups/500 g    fresh anchovies
1 cup/250 ml    wine vinegar
³/₄ cup/200 ml  native olive oil
                salt and pepper

**For the garnish:**
                cherry tomatoes
                chives
                lettuce leaves

The secret of this very popular dish of marinated anchovies is the quality of the olive oil. Back in Roman times, olive oil was an important commodity; indeed, it is still produced all over the country today. The oil is usually so pure and delicious that it can be drizzled generously over fish and salads without impairing the flavor. And, above all, it can be used to preserve foods such as sardines and anchovies.

Oil from the Ceuta region is particularly good. It is made from small, round olives with a thin skin. Half a spoonful is all that is needed to add a slightly fruit-acidic aroma to the marinade. Cherries or strawberries can be used instead of raspberries.

Anchovies are a firm fixture on menus all over Spain. These tiny herring are sold, preserved in salt or oil, in glass jars. Fresh anchovies have a silvery, shimmering skin and

shiny eyes. They need to be filleted before marinating so they are covered entirely by the marinade. With a little practice, you will soon be able to remove the head and main bones in one move. The fillets are rinsed, patted dry, and placed skin side down in a mold. They are then marinated in a mixture of water and vinegar, which ensures the flesh stays nice and firm. This marinade is poured away after 10 hours, and then the anchovy fillets are covered in olive oil and left for a further 3 hours. The small fish survive this marinating with no ill effects. Directly before serving they can be sprinkled with a little raspberry-flavored olive oil.

Stored in an airtight jar in the refrigerator, the raspberry oil will keep for about two weeks. It goes extremely well with salads, cold roast meats, and cold cuts.

Purée the raspberries and pass them through a sieve. Put 3 tbsp of this raspberry coulis into the olive oil, then pour into a small bottle.

Cut into the anchovies behind the head, and remove the head and main bone in one move. Carefully open out the fish and remove the insides. Rinse briefly under running cold water.

Put the anchovy fillets skin side down in a flat dish. Cover with water and the wine vinegar, and leave to marinate for 10 hours.

# Raspberry Oil

Remove the anchovies from the marinade and pat dry. Place in a dish, then season with salt and pepper, and pour over the olive oil. Chill for 3 hours.

Place the anchovies skin side down on paper towels, then leave for 10 minutes until some of the oil has been absorbed.

Now place the anchovies skin side up on plates. Garnish with cherry tomatoes, chives, and lettuce leaves. Drizzle generously with raspberry oil.

# Asparagus from

Preparation time: *30 minutes*
Cooking time: *25 minutes*
Difficulty: ★

**Serves 4**

| | |
|---|---|
| 1 lb 2 oz/500 g | fresh green asparagus |
| 1 lb 2 oz/500 g | fresh white asparagus |
| 4 | fresh eggs |

**For the sauce:**

| | |
|---|---|
| 2 | eggs |
| ¼ stick/30 g | butter |
| 1 tbsp/15 ml | sherry vinegar |
| pinch | ground paprika |
| | salt and pepper |

Fresh asparagus is available everywhere in Madrid from April to September. It is usually from Aranjuez, the old royal residence on the banks of the Tajo between Madrid and Toledo. Both green and white asparagus thrives in the fertile soils of the area.

This delicate vegetable was popular with the Greeks and Egyptians thousands of years ago. Clever Roman chefs found ways and means to grow the tender stalks, but after the fall of Rome it sank into oblivion until Louis XIV—whose favorite vegetable it was—started a veritable boom in the 17th century. He demanded to have the tender stems all year round, and so his gardener, La Quintinie, invented the greenhouse cultivation of this noble vegetable. When Louis's grandson, Bourbon King Philip V, ascended to the Spanish throne in 1700 he introduced asparagus to the Iberian Peninsula.

Formerly, the preference in Madrid was for a simple recipe, in which the eggs were cooked together with the asparagus. Creative chefs developed this further into a dish that was served with a sauce made of butter and eggs. Green asparagus must be plunged into iced water after cooking to help it retain its bright green color. It looks very pretty if the stalks are "tied" into small bundles with a strip of leek or chive.

The eggs are soft-boiled in their shells and plunged into iced water so that the white becomes firm but the yellow stays soft, oozing over the asparagus when the egg is cut. The sauce must be beaten very quickly with a balloon whisk over a low heat, otherwise the eggs will curdle and not blend with the butter. Whisk the ingredients over hot water until you have a smooth and velvety sauce that adheres to the back of the spoon.

*Peel the green and white asparagus with a vegetable peeler. Only the tips and about 2 in (5 cm) of the stalks are used for this recipe.*

*Blanch the green asparagus in boiling water for 2 minutes, and the white for about 8 minutes. As soon as it is cooked, plunge it into a bowl of iced water.*

*Slide the eggs into boiling water and boil for 3–4 minutes, then drop them in a bowl of iced water.*

# Aranjuez with Eggs

To make the sauce, place a bowl in a pot of hot water and beat the eggs. Add the butter, vinegar, ground paprika, salt, and pepper, then whisk well.

Whisk the sauce over hot water for about 10 minutes until it is smooth, bright orange-yellow in color, and has increased considerably in volume.

Bundle together the asparagus stalks and tie them together using, for example, strips of leek. Arrange on plates. Carefully peel the eggs, cut them in half, and place them next to the asparagus. Cover with the egg yolk and the sauce.

# Squid with

Preparation time: 40 minutes
Cooking time: 50 minutes
Difficulty: ✳

**Serves 4**

| | |
|---|---|
| 2¼ lb/1 kg | small squid |
| 2 | tomatoes |
| 1 | onion |
| 1 cup/250 ml | olive oil |
| 2 tbsp/30 ml | fish stock concentrate |
| 2 | bay leaves |
| 1 cup/250 ml | white wine |
| | salt and black pepper |

**For the potato crème:**

| | |
|---|---|
| 1 lb 2 oz/500 g | potatoes |
| 2 tbsp/30 ml | chicken stock |
| 1 cup/250 ml | cream |
| | salt |

This squid dish is made to a traditional recipe from the Bay of Vigo on the Galician coast. Fish and seafood have always been popular in this region, and they are eaten in a thousand variations.

When it is cooked in its ink, squid develops the most wonderful aroma. María Lourdes Fernández-Estevez serves it with creamy mashed potatoes, easy to make and a popular side dish everywhere in Spain. Squid is recognized by its oval, gray-brown body and its relatively large head, which has a total of ten tentacles—eight of which are short and two very long. The sack-shaped body with fins contains a hard white piece of calcium, the cuttlebone, which must be removed before cooking. Make sure when you are buying your squid that you are given one with the ink sac. When you are cleaning it, take care not to damage the ink sac.

Compared with other ten-tentacled cephalopods, squid are relatively small.

Bay leaf is a popular seasoning for fish dishes in Galicia. The aromatic, slightly bitter, leaf is used either whole or crumbled—but use it sparingly.

Potato crème is the ideal accompaniment to squid. The mild, creamy purée is made with cream. The potato, originally from South America, can be prepared in any number of ways, and has long been a staple in our diet. Stored in a cool, dry place, and out of the light, potatoes keep well. Choose smooth, firm tubers with no obvious sprouts. Surprise your guests with this original dish!

*Clean the squid and remove the cuttlebone. Remove the ink sac. Cut off the heads and tentacles.*

*Purée the tomatoes. Peel and finely chop the onion. Sauté the onion in hot olive oil. Add the tomato purée and stir well. Simmer gently for about 10 minutes.*

*Add the squid and stir well. Bring 2 cups (500 ml) water, the fish stock concentrate, and the bay leaves to the boil in a pot. Season with salt and pepper. Peel the potatoes, and cook in boiling water.*

# Potato Crème

Crush the ink sacs and add the ink to the squid.

Pour over the white wine. Bring to the boil, and add the seasoned fish stock. Simmer for about 40 minutes.

Mash the potatoes and work to a purée with the chicken stock. Heat over a low heat, and add the cream. Whisk with a balloon whisk. Boil briefly. Remove from the heat. Divide between the plates, and arrange the squid on the sauce.

# Paprika

Preparation time: 45 minutes
Chilling time: 2 hours
Cooking time: 30 minutes
Difficulty: ★

**Serves 4**

| | |
|---|---|
| 4 | eggplants |
| 4 | red bell peppers |
| 4 | green bell peppers |
| 4 | tomatoes |
| 1¼ cups/300 ml | olive oil |
| 2 tbsp/30 ml | sherry vinegar |
| 2 drops | Tabasco |
| | salt and pepper |

**For the garnish:**

chives
ground paprika
(optional)

**For serving:**
8 slices    baguette

Anyone who wants to discover Spain's gastronomy will find a wealth of aromas that have made their way into a number of simple, but very clever, recipes. Nothing is left to chance. This also applies to *escalivada*. The Spanish verb is *escalivar*, and means something along the lines of "peeling the skin from cooked vegetables." The classic vegetables for this Catalan recipe are eggplants, bell peppers, and onion, which are cut into quarters and roasted in their skins.

Whatever the season, *escalivada* is served cold. The vegetables are all arranged on a plate. Unlike other countries, where vegetables are usually served as a side dish, the Spanish like to eat it as a main dish. A plate of these broiled vegetables is therefore more suitable as a small, tasty appetizer.

Spain is now the world's leading exporter of olive oil. The main part of its more than 2 million acres (900,000 hectares) of olive oil groves is in Andalusia, but there are different varieties on the peninsula. The four main ones are Picual, Arbequina, Cornicabra, and Hojiblanca. There are six controlled marks of origin for Spanish olive oil—four Andalusian and two Catalan. As when making wine, the fruit for the oil is chosen with care. The bright yellow or greenish-shimmering oil is mild or spicy, and smells of milk, almonds, or citrus leaves. Each variety adds its own typical aroma to salads, marinade, meat, or fish sauces. To complement the flavor of his *escalivada*, Javier Valero uses a fruity, slightly dry, Catalan oil.

A tomato vinaigrette is the ideal garnish. A white wine from Penedés goes perfectly with this dish.

Pre-heat the oven to 350 °F/180 °C. Pierce the eggplants and bake with the bell peppers for 20–25 minutes, turning halfway through. Meanwhile, pour boiling water over the tomatoes, remove the skins and seeds, then cut into quarters. Set aside.

Place the broiled vegetables in a sieve and cover with plastic wrap; chill for 2 hours.

When cold, remove the skins from the vegetables. Cut into the bell peppers, and remove the seeds.

# Escalivada

Cut the bell peppers and eggplants into strips.

To make the vinaigrette, purée two of the quartered tomatoes, and add 1 cup (250 ml) olive oil and vinegar. Season with salt, pepper, and Tabasco.

Arrange the vegetable strips in a grid on a plate, and sprinkle with vinaigrette. Garnish with the remaining tomato pieces and chives, and dust with a little ground paprika if desired. Serve with golden-yellow toasted bread, sprinkled with olive oil.

# Sardine

| Preparation time: | 30 minutes |
| Marinating: | half a day |
| Cooking time: | 10 minutes |
| Difficulty: | ★ |

**Serves 4**

| 24 | large sardines |
| sprigs | fresh thyme |
| sprigs | fresh rosemary |
| | fresh bay leaves |
| pinch | ground nutmeg |

| 2 cups/500 ml | olive oil |
| 3 | tomatoes |
| dash | sherry vinegar |
| 2 tbsp | flat-leaf parsley |
| | salt and pepper |

Centuries ago, people who liked eating grilled food had the brilliant idea to slide it onto small sticks, or skewers. And so *espetones* were born. Even today, fishermen and other coastal dwellers skewer five or six sardines on a piece of reed, stick it in the sand, and cook the fish over an open wood fire. Fresh from the skewer, they are the greatest delicacy. Of course, specialists position their skewers according to the wind so that the aroma of the fish is not affected by the smoke.

Because not all of us have a beach close by, our chef thought of something else. He threads five sardines onto thin wooden skewers, and bakes them in the oven. Professional chefs usually use a so-called salamander, but most of us do not have one of these appliances, with their impressive top heat, in our kitchen.

Sardines from the Atlantic or Mediterranean are very popular on the Iberian Peninsula. They got their name from the island of Sardinia, where they were already a popular delicacy in Roman antiquity. Today, they are found in vast shoals all over the Mediterranean. Spanish gourmets like to eat them grilled or broiled, usually with a little olive oil and some aromatic herbs.

If the sardines are on the big side, they should be cleaned and boned. To do so, cut into the belly with scissors or a small sharp knife. Very small sardines are best left whole.

*Cut off the tip of the tail from each sardine and remove the scales. Cut into the belly with scissors, remove the insides, and wash.*

*Place the sardines in an ovenproof dish, and season with salt and pepper. Add the thyme, rosemary, bay leaves, and nutmeg, plus 1 cup (250 ml) of olive oil, then marinate for half a day.*

*Slide five of the marinated sardines onto a skewer and put them back in the same dish to broil in the oven for 10 minutes, turning them once.*

# Skewers

Pour boiling water over the tomatoes and plunge them into cold water. Remove the skins, cut the tomatoes into quarters, and remove the seeds. Chop into small pieces.

Pour a little vinegar over the juices in the ovenproof dish. Whisk together the remaining olive oil, salt, and pepper with a fork.

Add the chopped tomatoes and chopped parsley to this sauce. Arrange the sardine skewers on plates, and pour over the sauce. Garnish with rosemary, thyme, and bay leaves.

# Vegetable Stew

Preparation time: 35 minutes
Cooking time: 25 minutes
Difficulty: ☆

**Serves 4**

| | |
|---|---|
| 10 oz/250 g | green beans |
| 1 | carrot |
| 1 | mangold leaf |
| 10 oz/250 g | cauliflower |
| 10 oz/250 g | green asparagus |
| 1 tsp | baking soda |

| | |
|---|---|
| 2 | artichokes |
| 1 clove | garlic |
| 4 tbsp/60 ml | olive oil |
| 2 slices | Iberian ham (Pata negra) |
| | coarse sea salt |

**For the lechada:**

| | |
|---|---|
| 1 tbsp/15 g | flour |
| 1 tbsp/15 ml | olive oil |
| 1 | lemon, squeezed |
| | salt |

This vegetable stew with ham is served warm, and is a real spring meal. A specialty from Navarre, it is greatly prized all over Spain and part of the culinary heritage of the Iberian Peninsula. It is easy to prepare, and makes the most of the vegetables grown around Navarre. The so-called Ribera, which simply means "valley," is famous for its vegetables. Vegetables are the main ingredient in the native cuisine, which is famous far and wide for its finesse.

Thanks to a clever irrigation system, which dates back to the times when Arabs ruled over southern Spain, vegetables thrive particularly well in this region—including, and in particular, green beans and mangold. The vegetables for this *menestra* (stew) are blanched briefly in salted water so they stay crisp. Allow 10 minutes for the beans, 12 for the white of the mangold leaves and the carrots, and 8 minutes for the cauliflower and asparagus.

The secret to this extremely healthy dish is the green asparagus. It is the pride of the vegetable farmers of Navarre, who still use the traditions of their ancestors to grow it. According to the chef, green asparagus is far superior to white. Make sure the tips are still firmly closed. Wrapped in a damp cloth in the refrigerator, asparagus will keep for three to four days. Rinse briefly under running water before cooking. Peel the stalks from the tip down, and cut off the woody stalk.

The artichokes are cooked in a *lechada*—a combination of flour, lemon juice, olive oil, and salt, which prevents them from turning black. Drain the artichokes when cooked and add them to the stew.

*Trim the beans, carrot, mangold, cauliflower, and asparagus and—with the exception of the cauliflower—cut into small pieces. Blanch each type of vegetable separately in salted water. Add the baking soda to the water for the asparagus.*

*Cut off the leaves of the artichokes until only the hearts are left, and cut them in half. In a pot, heat 1½ cups (350 ml) water with the flour, olive oil, lemon juice, and salt. Cook the artichoke hearts in the lechada for 20 minutes.*

*Peel the garlic and chop very finely. Sauté in olive oil.*

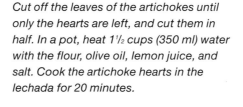

# with Ham

Drain the vegetables and add to the garlic. Sauté for 2 minutes.

Sieve the lechada, pour over the vegetables, and simmer for 2 minutes.

Slice the ham very thinly, and sauté in a little olive oil. Arrange the vegetables on plates. Sprinkle with the ham strips, and pour a little of the sauce around them.

# Diced Bread

Preparation time: 15 minutes
Standing time for
  the bread: 12 hours
Cooking time: 15 minutes
Difficulty: ☆

**Serves 4**

| | |
|---|---|
| 3 lb 5 oz/1.5 kg | white bread |
| 3 | chorizo sausages |

| | |
|---|---|
| 12 oz/300 g | bacon slab |
| 2¼ lb/1 kg | grapes |
| | a little olive oil |
| 6 cloves | garlic |
| 2 tsp | ground paprika (pimientón) |
| | salt |

This very simple dish is typical of Castile and the Estremadura. Grape pickers meet in September to enjoy this traditional specialty. The olive oil, chorizo, bacon, garlic, ground paprika, and salt are what give the bread its special flavor. Juicy grapes are the perfect complement. *Migas*—which translates as breadcrumbs—has been prepared in many different ways for thousands of years. The original inhabitants of the Iberian Peninsula prepared a dish of stale bread and fat. Shepherds and muleteers did not need to be near a town or village to enjoy this simple, rustic dish. Over the course of time the dish was incorporated in Spanish cuisine, and each region has developed its own variation.

According to purists, the bread for *migas* needs to be very dry and ideally four days old. The chef recommends soaking it in a little water and leaving it to stand for at least twelve hours before preparing the dish. This prevents the bread from absorbing too much fat. The extremely popular *migas ruleras* are served with grapes. The texture of the grape skin and sweetness or acidity of the flesh are determined by the quality and origin. The season for red grapes is from August to November.

Make sure that the grapes are fresh and ripe. Use them at room temperature so the full flavor and aroma can develop, and remember to wash them thoroughly. Alberto Herráiz recommends using sweet melon instead of grapes in summer. Some families serve dried sardines or fried eggs with their *migas*.

*The evening before, cut the bread into slices, remove the crusts, and dice the bread. Place the bread cubes in a bowl and sprinkle with a little water. Cover with a clean cloth and leave to stand for 12 hours.*

*Slice the chorizo and dice the bacon. Remove the grapes from the stalks and wash them thoroughly.*

*Heat a little olive oil in a skillet, and fry the bread cubes. Then add the sliced garlic, and the diced bacon. Combine well and cook, then remove from the skillet and set aside.*

# with Grapes

Sprinkle the ground paprika into the skillet and stir with a spatula.

Add the softened bread cubes. Sauté, stirring continuously, until golden and crispy. Season with salt.

Add the sliced sausage and diced bacon, and reheat gently over a low heat. Arrange the migas on a plate, and garnish with the grapes.

# Vegetable

Preparation time:    20 minutes
Cooking time:        50 minutes
Difficulty:          ★

**Serves 4**

| | |
|---|---|
| 4 oz/100 g | baby fava beans (broad beans), washed |
| ½ lb/200 g | cauliflower florets |
| 4 | artichokes |
| ½ | leek |
| 1 | red bell pepper |

| | |
|---|---|
| 1 | carrot |
| 1 | zucchini |
| 3 | mangold leaves |
| 1 | ripe tomato |
| 3 cloves | garlic |
| 7 tbsp/100 ml | olive oil |
| 1 tsp | ground paprika |
| 1½ cups/350 g | rice (ideally "Bomba") |
| 8 cups/2 l | chicken stock |
| pinch | saffron threads |
| | salt |

Vegetable paella is not really a traditional Spanish dish, but it is something that is enjoyed by many families in the Valencia region. Oscar Torrijos has been lovingly making his own version for 30 years.

Rice has been grown in the marshy region of Albufera near Valencia since the Middle Ages. This is where paella, the pride of all Valencians, hails from. The word "paella" referred originally to the large, shallow pan with two handles in which rice, fish, vegetables, or seafood were prepared. Paella used to be served only on high days and holidays, and was usually eaten outside.

Today, paella may be made from a huge variety of ingredients. Oscar Torrijos recommends bomba rice, which is grown near Valencia. Its advantage is that the grains increase three- to fourfold during cooking without bursting.

They absorb the stock well, and develop an incomparable aroma. One kilogram of rice is enough for 10 to 12 people. In Albufera, rice is harvested in September and October. The rice is then dried, peeled and polished. The grains are considered "young" until the following May. The cooking time for paella is 18 to 20 minutes. Special skillets are available, but a normal skillet or even a casserole will also do well.

The vegetables can be chosen according to what is in season. In Valencia, vegetables come from the Huerta region, a vast fruit and vegetable growing area, where artichokes, bell peppers and chiles, carrots, cabbages, eggplants, potatoes, tomatoes, mangold, onion, beans, and many more varieties are cultivated. Such abundance stimulates creativity, which is confirmed most wonderfully by Oscar Torrijos' paella.

*Trim the beans, and cut the cauliflower into small rosettes. Trim the artichokes, and cut into pieces.*

*Prepare the remaining vegetables as follows: cut the leek, bell pepper, carrot and zucchini into 2 in (4 cm) pieces. Thinly slice the mangold. Skin the tomato, cut into quarters, then remove the seeds. Peel and chop the garlic.*

*Combine the vegetables in a bowl. Heat the olive oil in a paella pan, then sauté the vegetables. Add the ground paprika. Continue cooking for about 5 minutes, stirring continuously.*

# Paella

As soon as the vegetables start to turn brown, add the rice and stir until it becomes transparent.

Pour over the chicken stock, and bring to the boil.

Season with saffron and salt, and simmer gently for 20 minutes, stirring continuously. Finally, put the paella in the oven for 8 minutes, and serve very hot.

# Clams with

Preparation time: 20 minutes
Cooking time: 15 minutes
Difficulty: ✶

**Serves 4**

| | |
|---|---|
| 24 large | clams |
| 3 | eggs |
| 2 | scallions (spring onion) |
| 7 tbsp/100 ml | olive oil |
| 1 | lemon |
| ⅓ cup/80 g | trout caviar |
| | coarse and fine salt |
| | pepper |

Many Spanish connoisseurs eat their clams—known as *almejas*—raw. As with oysters, they simply open the shell and suck out the clam. However, Oscar Torrijos suggests a version that could easily be on the menu of any leading restaurant. It combines three components that are not usually used together: broiled clams, *gribiche* sauce, and trout caviar.

Thanks to its location on the Mediterranean, the province of Valencia offers a wealth of fish and seafood, from mussels, oysters, and scallops to clams. The latter are double shelled with a rock-hard shell and gray to dark orange flesh. In Valencia they are eaten from September until the end of April. Excellent *almejas* also come from other coastal regions of Spain. Those from Carril on the Galician Atlantic coast are considered particularly flavorsome.

For this recipe, Oscar Torrijos was inspired by a typical Valencian cooking method. Valencians like their food as natural as possible, preferably *a la plancha*—that is, cooked on a red-hot griddle brushed with olive oil, whether fish and mussels or vegetables and meat. The food retains its natural flavor and nutritional value. Remember, though, that the cooking time for mussels cooked this way is extremely short. Place the clams in their shells on the hot skillet, and remove them from the heat as soon as the liquid inside them starts to bubble.

You can add any herbs you like to the *gribiche* sauce—such as parsley, chervil, or basil. Trout caviar, gray mullet roe, or herring roe are the ideal accompaniment.

*Place the clams on a chopping board. Cut through the adductor muscle with a sharp knife and open the shell.*

*Sprinkle coarse salt over the bottom of a skillet and heat. Place the clams on the layer of salt in the hot skillet, and broil for 2 minutes.*

*Boil the eggs for 6 minutes. Peel the white part of the scallion and cut into rings. Cover with water, then boil over a high heat for 5 minutes.*

# Trout Caviar

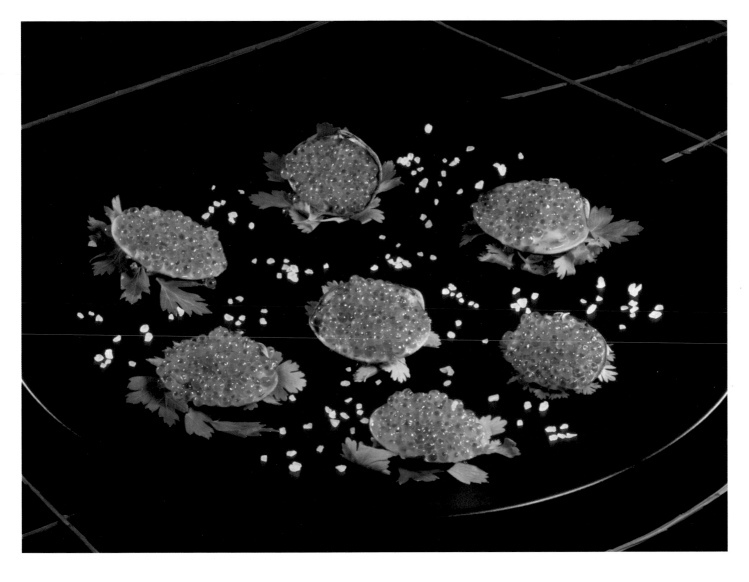

Drain the scallions and put them in a blender with the boiled, chopped egg yolks. Then pour over the olive oil and purée until well blended and light yellow in color.

Season with salt and pepper. Add the juice of the lemon, and stir well. Add a little of the green part of the scallion, finely chopped.

Arrange the half shells on a serving dish. Spoon some of the sauce into each one, and top with the trout caviar.

# Patatas

Preparation time: 25 minutes
Cooking time: 50 minutes
Difficulty: ★

**Serves 4**

| | |
|---|---|
| 6 medium | potatoes |
| 1¼ cups /150 g | flour |
| 2 | eggs |
| 2 cloves | garlic |

| | |
|---|---|
| 1 | onion |
| 4 cups/1 l | chicken stock (instant) |
| 10 | parsley stalks |
| 2–3 | chives |
| | salt and pepper |

Potatoes used to be on the menu every day in Spain, and so chefs devised a number of extravagant dishes for variety. One was *Patatas a la importancia*: slices of potato coated in egg and flour, which are first fried and then cooked in a tasty stock. This dish is on the menu in countless restaurants today. Potatoes originally came from Peru. The Incas cultivated them almost 3,000 years ago. Known to them as *papas*, the tuber came to Galicia with the returning Spanish conquerors in about 1570. However, to begin with it was not well received in Spain, the South of France, or Italy. For a long time it was used as animal fodder. But finally, in the 19th century, it was accepted in the kitchen.

Make sure that the potatoes are a firm-cooking variety, so they do not disintegrate in the stock. To coat them, Julio Reoyo cuts them into slices, seasons them with salt and pepper, then coats both sides in flour on a plate. Wait a moment until moisture starts to appear on the surface, then coat them in flour again so it adheres better while they are frying. Gently shake the potato slices to remove any excess flour.

The potato slices must not touch each other while they are frying. Each portion will take about 5 minutes to cook. Use a spatula to remove the potatoes from the hot oil, then continue cooking them in a clear chicken stock, which you can enhance with white wine and saffron threads. These delicious *patatas a la importancia* are ideal either as an appetizer or an entrée, maybe as a side dish with salmon slices or perhaps roast meat.

*Peel the potatoes and cut into ⅙ in/5 mm slices. Wash, and pat dry with paper towels.*

*Sprinkle the flour on a plate. Season the potato slices with salt and pepper, and coat well with the flour.*

*Beat the eggs and dip the potato slices in the eggs.*

# a la Importancia

Deep-fry the potatoes in portions in very hot oil for 5 minutes. Chop the garlic and onion, and sauté in hot oil for 5 minutes. Add 1 tbsp (15 g) of flour and stir well. Pour over the stock, then bring to the boil.

Shake any excess off the potato slices, then place the slices in the stock.

Chop the parsley and chives, then add to the potatoes. Press the potatoes down in the stock with the back of the spatula. Simmer gently for 30 minutes.

# Pisto

Preparation time:     *35 minutes*
Cooking time:     *35 minutes*
Difficulty:     ✲

**Serves 4**

| | |
|---|---|
| 2 | onions |
| 2 | green bell peppers |
| 12 oz/300 g | tomatoes |
| 12 oz/300 g | zucchini |

| | |
|---|---|
| 1 cup/250 ml | olive oil |
| 8 | eggs |
| 4 slices | white bread |
| | salt |
| | white pepper (optional) |

**For the garnish (optional):**

| | |
|---|---|
| 1 | dried red chile |
| strips | zucchini skin |

The Basque country on the Atlantic coast has developed an extensive repertoire of tasty dishes. The Basques are proud of their heritage, and of their reputation as connoisseurs. From simple *pintxo* and other tapas served at the bar and eaten "in the hand," to extremely lavish traditional dishes, Basque cuisine always reveals its wholly independent character.

*Pisto a la bilbaina* is a popular warm appetizer. As the name suggests, the dish—which is similar to the Tunisian *chakchouka*—is typical of the province of Bilbao. It is easy to make, and is a refreshing appetizer in summer when bell peppers, zucchini, and tomatoes are abundant on the markets. Made with generous quantities of olive oil, it is combined with beaten eggs at the end. *Pisto* is a light dish, easily digestible thanks to the zucchini, with plenty of liquid, and low in calories. The zucchini should be small and a standard dark green in color. This vegetable from the New World is now a firm fixture in Mediterranean cuisine.

For almost two centuries tomatoes were believed to be poisonous, but they were eventually accepted and are now an essential part of Mediterranean cuisine. Almost 4 million tons/3.6 million metric tonnes of the fruit are produced on the Iberian Peninsula every year. Tomatoes should be firm and fleshy with a fine aroma. Chef uses green bell peppers for this dish, which have the added advantage of keeping well. The aroma is slightly drier and stronger than that of red bell peppers, and therefore it goes extremely well with this dish.

Bread sautéed in olive oil is an excellent accompaniment to *pisto a la bilbaina*, which is excellent as an appetizer or entrée.

*Peel the onions. Wash the bell peppers, tomatoes, and zucchini. Peel a few strips of skin off one of the zucchini using a vegetable peeler, and set aside. Roughly chop the vegetables.*

*Heat 7 tbsp (100 ml) of olive oil, and sauté the bell pepper and onions. Cover and simmer for about 10 minutes, stirring occasionally with a wooden spoon.*

*Add the chopped tomatoes and zucchini, season well with salt and pepper, and stir. Continue to simmer for 15 minutes.*

# a la Bilbaina

Beat the eggs in a bowl.

Spoon the vegetables over the beaten egg with a skimmer. Sauté the bread in 7 tbsp (100 ml) olive oil, then set aside.

Heat the remainder of the olive oil in a large pot until very hot, then pour in the egg and vegetable mixture. Stir with a wooden spatula until it sets. Arrange the pisto on plates with the bread. Garnish with strips of chile and zucchini peel.

# Scallops with

Preparation time: 50 minutes
Cooking time: 30 minutes
Difficulty: ★

**Serves 4**

**Vegetables for rice and stock:**

| | |
|---|---|
| 1 cup/250 g | peas |
| 1 cup/250 g | fava beans (broad beans) |
| 1 | carrot |
| 1 | shallot |
| 1 | onion |
| 1 stalk | celery |
| 1 | zucchini |
| 1 | tomato |

**For the vegetable rice:**

| | |
|---|---|
| 4 tbsp/60 ml | olive oil |
| 3 sprigs | parsley |
| ³/₄ cup/200 g | rice |
| ³/₄ cup/200 ml | white wine |
| 3 tbsp/45 g | grated parmesan |

**For the scallops:**

| | |
|---|---|
| 16 | scallops |
| | a little olive oil |
| | salt and white pepper |

**For the garnish (optional):**

| | |
|---|---|
| | fresh basil leaves |

Scallops from Galicia are famed for their quality. Traditionally, they are baked in the oven *a la marinera* (with white wine and onions), but the delicate seafood is also ideal for many other cooking methods. To preserve the incomparable aroma, María Lourdes Fernández-Estevez recommends cooking them *a la plancha*—that is, frying them briefly. This clever, well-planned recipe includes creamy vegetable rice as the perfect accompaniment. It is quick to prepare, and tastes wonderful.

Ever since the Middle Ages scallops have been closely associated with Saint James and Santiago de Compostela, because the shells were the symbol of the Jacobean pilgrims. It is said that at the beginning of the 9th century, a hermit, guided by a strange star, found the grave of James the Apostle close to the Galician town. A magnificent Christian cathedral was built there, which is still a destination for many pilgrimages today.

Scallops from the coast of Galicia are known for their firm, snowy-white flesh and delicate aroma. They are caught between October and May. The cooking time is very short: in our recipe, they are cooked in a typically Spanish method *a la plancha* so they keep their fine shape and structure.

This spring-like dish is served with plenty of vegetables. Celery, onions, shallots, fava beans, zucchini, tomatoes, and peas create a beautiful harmony of colors with the rice—similar to that of an Italian risotto. The vegetable rice is seasoned with white wine, which goes perfectly with the scallops. The parmesan is a clever touch: this king of Italian hard cheeses adds a fruity piquant aroma to the dish. Scallops with rice are ideal as an appetizer and as an entrée. Serve with a dish of vegetables.

*To make the vegetable rice, trim the peas and fava beans. Peel or wash the carrot, shallot, onion, and celery; wash the zucchini and tomato. Chop all the vegetables very finely, setting aside 1¹/₄ cups (300 g).*

*Make a stock with the remaining vegetables and simmer for about 20 minutes. Heat the olive oil in a large pot, then sauté the diced vegetables and chopped parsley for about 5 minutes.*

*Add the rice and fry, stirring continuously.*

# Vegetable Rice

Pour over the white wine, and stir. Strain the vegetable stock through a sieve.

Put a little clear stock in the pot. Simmer for about 10 minutes, stirring continuously, gradually adding the remainder of the stock. Season with salt and pepper, and sprinkle over the parmesan.

Salt the scallops, and sprinkle with olive oil. Sauté in a hot metal pot for about 2 minutes. Arrange on plates, and serve with a shaped portion of vegetable rice. Garnish with basil leaves.

# Salmorejo

| Preparation time: | 15 minutes |
| Cooking time for the eggs: | 10 minutes |
| Difficulty: | ☆ |

**Serves 4**

| 2 | eggs |
| 2¼ lb/1 kg | ripe tomatoes |
| 6 cloves | garlic |

| 12 oz/300 g | bread |
| ¾ cup/200 ml | native olive oil |
| 7 tbsp/100 ml | sherry vinegar |
| 6 oz/150 g | smoked ham |
| | salt |

*Salmorejo de Córdoba* is basically a cold purée of fresh tomatoes and garlic. The difference between it and gazpacho is that the latter is made of various vegetables flavored with cumin and paprika, and is thinner in texture. In Andalusia, *salmorejo* is often served as a topping for bread rather than as a meal in itself. It is particularly refreshing on a hot summer's day. During the traditional parades, the *Romerías* (the village dwellers) prepare *salmorejo* at home, then share it at the festivities.

It is essential that the tomatoes for this dish are red and soft. Strictly speaking, they should be crushed in a mortar and pestle with the garlic, but a kitchen blender is used in Córdoba today. The dish contains plenty of garlic, but you can use less if you prefer. However, the indigestible green core should be removed. If you add a little coarse salt, you will find it easier to crush the garlic; the salt helps the garlic to adhere to the bottom of the mortar and prevents it from escaping as you crush it.

The chef recommends a high quality, finely grained white bread, ideally baked the day before. The quality of the bread is essential, because it adds its velvety consistency to the dish. In Spain there is a rustic, round variety of bread called *candeal*, which is ideal.

The final step in the preparation is to add oil and vinegar to the *salmorejo*. The vinegar should only be added just before it is served; otherwise it will become too acid. José-Ignacio Herráiz garnishes the dish with hard-boiled eggs and smoked ham, but you could also use tuna, slices of sour gherkin, mint leaves, or grated cheese.

*Boil the eggs for 10 minutes, then plunge them into cold water and peel. Wash and dry the tomatoes, cut out the stalks, and cut the tomatoes into quarters.*

*Peel the garlic and crush with a pinch of salt in a mortar and pestle.*

*Put the garlic in the mixing bowl of the blender. Add the tomatoes, and process.*

# de Córdoba

Cut the crust off the bread, and chop the bread roughly. Moisten with water in a bowl, then crush with a fork. Put the bowl in the blender with the tomatoes.

Run the appliance until the mixture becomes a smooth pink purée.

Add the oil and vinegar, and season to taste. Garnish the salmorejo with quartered eggs and strips of ham.

# Vegetable and

| | |
|---|---|
| Preparation time: | 30 minutes |
| Cooking time: | 40 minutes |
| Difficulty: | ✶ |

**Serves 6**

| | |
|---|---|
| 2¼ lb/1 kg | potatoes |
| 8 oz/200 g | onions |
| 2 small | zucchini |
| 4 tbsp/60 ml | olive oil |
| 10 | eggs |
| 1 cup/200 g | cooked shrimp |
| 1 tsp | salt |
| ½ tsp | pepper |

All those whose eyes sparkle at the mention of the word "picnic," but have had more than their fair share of potato chips and sandwiches, will love this appetizing tortilla, which is eaten warm and made to an old Seville family recipe. A tortilla is a kind of omelet, full to bursting with eggs, potatoes, and onions, as well as other ingredients that are left to the chef's imagination.

In Spanish households, the eggs for the tortilla are whipped up on a Saturday night. The tortilla is then baked at the last minute on Sunday, and taken to the beach. The potatoes are peeled, and then diced immediately without patting them dry. Use large potatoes for a truly authentic Spanish touch. The onions and potatoes are cooked in a covered skillet together, making sure they don't turn brown.

Zucchini do not take long to cook if they are to retain some crunch. Large or small, they contain plenty of water,

so they are cooked uncovered to enable some of the liquid to evaporate. Instead of zucchini you could also use eggplant, mushrooms, or tomatoes. For a particularly aromatic tortilla, save the vegetable juices and drizzle them over the tortilla when you turn it. Whatever your preference, one thing always remains the same: the eggs are beaten with a fork.

The olive oil should be very hot, but the tortilla must not burn. Shake the skillet a little to blend the contents well. When you want to turn the tortilla over, place a large plate face down on top of the skillet, turn everything upside down so the tortilla ends up on the plate, then slide the tortilla back into the skillet. As it sets, the tortilla should double in volume.

*Peel the potatoes and onions. Cut the onions and zucchini into three lengthwise and, holding them together with your fingers, cut them crosswise into ¾ in (2 cm) cubes.*

*Fry the potatoes in 1 tbsp of hot olive oil. Add the onions, and combine well. Cover and simmer gently for 15 minutes. Add the zucchini, and cook uncovered for a further 15 minutes. Drain the vegetables in a sieve.*

*Put the cooked vegetables in a bowl, and set aside. Crack the eggs into a large bowl and, using a fork, whisk them gently, then more briskly for 10 minutes.*

# Shrimp Tortilla

Peel and halve the shrimp. Combine with the vegetables, and add everything to the beaten egg. Season with salt and pepper, and stir well.

Heat the remainder of the olive oil in a large, deep skillet, and add the mixture at once. Smooth the surface and fry uncovered over a high heat for 5 minutes.

When the tortilla begins to set, put a plate on top and remove from the heat. Turn the tortilla over, then put the skillet back on the heat and slide the tortilla back into the skillet. Cook over a low heat for a further 5 minutes. Serve warm.

# Xatonada

| Preparation time: | 30 minutes |
| --- | --- |
| Soaking time stockfish: | 48 hours |
| Soaking time pimiento ñora: | 2 hours |
| Chilling time: | 1 hour |
| Cooking time: | 25 minutes |
| Difficulty: | ★ |

**Serves 4**

| 8 oz/200 g | stockfish |
| --- | --- |
| 1 head | curly endive |
| 12 | anchovy fillets (glass) |
| 3/4 cup/200 g | tuna (canned) |
| 30 | black olives |

**For the romesco sauce:**

| 1 | dried red paprika (pimiento ñora) |
| --- | --- |
| 3 cloves | garlic |
| 1 1/4 cups/300 ml | olive oil |
| 4 tsp/20 g | skinned almonds |
| 4 tsp/20 g | skinned hazelnuts |
| 3 | ripe tomatoes |
| 2 slices | bread |
| 6 1/2 tbsp/100 ml | red wine vinegar salt |

*Xatonada* is from Catalonia—from the region around Tarragona, to be precise. Whether this popular salad actually originates from Sitges or Vilanova is hotly contested between the two rival towns. Competitions take place regularly at public festivals to see whose is the best *Xatonada*. Pep Masiques' version is more of a winter dish, because that is when curly endive is widely available.

Soak the stockfish (dried salted cod) in water for 24 to 48 hours. The water should be changed frequently to rinse away the salt. Then pull off the skin and carefully remove all the bones. Finally, break the stockfish into small pieces.

The romesco sauce is bound with almonds, bread, and hazelnuts, and is an ancient dish from the mountain country

of Catalonia. It is particularly tasy with stockfish and seafood. It is named after the romesco pepper. This vegetable, which was brought from America to Europe in the 16th century, is often called *pimiento ñora*. The small, round pod develops an exceptionally spicy aroma without bite. It is garnet red when dried. Remove the stalk and seeds before soaking.

Blanch the almonds before using them. Put them in a pot of boiling water and boil them until the skins come off. Then drain them, place on a cloth, and rub thoroughly. If necessary, remove the skin with a sharp knife. Rinse the anchovies, and remove the bones if necessary. Sauté the tomatoes for the sauce last, as they create lots of juice that blends with the oil.

*Soak the stockfish for 48 hours. Remove the skin and bones, and break the fish into pieces using your fingers.*

*Soak the dried paprika in a bowl of cold water for 2 hours. Then cut the pod open and scoop out the pulp with a teaspoon. Peel and slice the garlic.*

*Fry the garlic in 3/4 cup (200 ml) of very hot olive oil for 5 minutes until golden. Remove, and set aside. Fry the almonds in the same skillet for 5 minutes. Set aside. Repeat the process with the hazelnuts, quartered tomatoes, and bread.*

Place the ingredients in the mixing bowl of your blender, and add the paprika pulp. Blend until smooth.

Add the remainder of the olive oil and the vinegar to the sauce, and stir again. Pour the romesco sauce into a bowl, then chill for 1 hour. Season if required.

To prepare the salad, wash and spin dry the endive. Cut out the core with a sharp knife so the leaves come loose. Put the salad leaves in a bowl, and arrange the stockfish, tuna, anchovies, olives, and romesco sauce on top.

Soups

# Gazpacho

Preparation time: 20 minutes
Roasting pine nuts: 5 minutes
Difficulty: ✶

**Serves 4**

| | |
|---|---|
| 4 slices | white bread |
| 4 cloves | garlic |
| 2 | red bell peppers |
| 4 | large cucumbers |
| 15 | ripe tomatoes |

| | |
|---|---|
| 6 oz/150 g | onion |
| ¾ cup/200 g | pine nuts |
| pinch | cumin (optional) |
| | a little virgin olive oil |
| | a little sherry vinegar |
| 6½ tbsp/100 ml | cream (optional) |
| | salt |

In 1967, José-Ignacio Herráiz's mother Nelia opened a restaurant in the ancient city of Cuenca, in the province of La Mancha. Her son has now taken it on—and inherited Mom's delicious recipe for Andalusian gazpacho. The cold tomato soup is extremely popular all over Spain, particularly in summer, when it is an almost permanent fixture on the menu in restaurants and homes. In fact, it is also popular as a refreshing drink with lunch.

Although the original recipe calls for cumin as a seasoning, our chef prefers to leave it out because he finds it can dominate. The toasted pine nuts are what make José-Ignacio Herráiz's version of the recipe so special. They add a slightly resinous touch to the gazpacho as well as making it a bit thicker. The chef sometimes adds a little cream to the cold soup to blend the various flavors.

Different varieties of tomato may be used for gazpacho, but they must be fully ripe. Deep red plum tomatoes, grown on the Canary Islands, are the preferred choice in Spain.

When preparing the cucumbers for this soup, do remember to remove the indigestible seeds by scooping them out with a teaspoon. Our chef sprinkles the cucumbers with salt to remove some of the liquid. He then rinses them under running water before combining them with the other ingredients. The gazpacho is seasoned with olive oil and sherry vinegar. The latter is made from the sweet Andalusian wine of the same name that comes from the region of Cádiz, and in particular Jerez de la Frontera, Sanlúcar de Barrameda, and El Puerto de Santa María. Serve gazpacho well chilled, accompanied by a colorful selection of finely chopped vegetables.

*Trim the crust off the bread. Moisten the remainder of the bread and crush with a fork until it is fairly soft in consistency. Peel the garlic.*

*Halve the bell peppers, and remove the pith and seeds. Chop the flesh into pieces. Peel the cucumbers, cut them in half lengthwise, and then into slices. Skin the tomatoes and onions, and cut them into quarters, keeping some for garnish.*

*Dry roast the pine nuts in a skillet for 5 minutes until golden.*

# a la Nelia

Blend the bell peppers with a little water. Add the cucumber, tomatoes, and onions, followed by the pine nuts, garlic, and cumin if used. Work until smooth and well blended.

Add the softened bread, and blend.

Season with a little olive oil, sherry vinegar, and salt, and pulse again briefly. Pour the gazpacho into soup bowls. Garnish with chopped tomatoes, onions, cucumber, and bell pepper. Adding cream to this soup is optional.

# Catalan

Preparation time: 30 minutes
Cooking time: 1 hour
Difficulty: ★

**Serves 4**

| | |
|---|---|
| 2½ tbsp/40 g | dried porcini |
| 1 cup/250 g | fresh chanterelles |
| ¾ cup/200 ml | olive oil |
| 2 | onions |
| 2 | leeks |
| 3 | ripe tomatoes |

| | |
|---|---|
| 2 cups/500 ml | chicken stock |
| 2 slices | white bread |
| | salt |

**For the picada:**

| | |
|---|---|
| 2 cloves | garlic |
| pinch/0.6 g | saffron |
| 4 tsp/20 g | toasted almonds |
| pinch | salt |

Mushroom gatherers take to the forests of Catalonia in September, so it is hardly surprising that there should be an abundance of recipes for mushroom soup. This soup is a popular everyday dish that owes its full spiciness not only to the mushrooms in it, but also to the addition of onions, tomatoes, and leeks.

Pep Masiques prefers two highly aromatic mushroom varieties: porcini and chanterelles. The latter grow in mixed forests from the end of May to October, at the foot of oaks, chestnuts, and walnut trees, as well as around conifers. The aroma of this mild, slightly peppery, mushroom is reminiscent of peaches, or apricots.

In contrast to the chanterelles, which are used fresh, for this recipe Pep Masiques prefers to use dried porcini. These tiny, gray-pink mushrooms have a slightly cone-shaped top and a tough inedible stalk. They grow in abundance in fields and meadows, and by the side of the road, from spring until fall. Remember to drain the mushrooms in a sieve after cooking to remove any excess oil. Instead of using bought chicken stock, you can also "stretch" this soup by using your own chicken stock, which you can make from chicken bones and vegetables.

For the *picada* (spiced paste), chef puts the mortar on the kitchen towel and wraps the ends around the pestle to prevent the contents from escaping. Some families simply purée the soup, but purists insist on straining it through a sieve for an even finer, more homogeneous consistency. If you find the soup too thick, thin it with a little hot water or stock.

*Soak the porcini in warm water for 5 minutes and drain. Wash the chanterelles and cut into pieces, reserving 2–3 for garnish.*

*Heat ⅔ cup (150 ml) olive oil in a skillet and sauté the porcini for 5 minutes. Then add the chanterelles, and season with salt. Simmer for 10 minutes until the liquid has evaporated. Drain the mushrooms.*

*Peel and finely chop the onions. Sauté in the remainder of the oil with the finely sliced leeks for 15–20 minutes. Cut the tomatoes into quarters, and add. Simmer for a further 8–10 minutes.*

# Mushroom Soup

Add the mushrooms, pour over the stock, and stir well. Bring to the boil.

Place the bread slices in the soup, then simmer for 5 minutes.

For the picada, peel and coarsely chop the garlic. Then crush in the mortar with saffron, almonds, and a pinch of salt. Add this paste to the soup, and blend with a hand blender. Serve garnished with fried chanterelles.

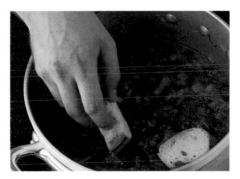

# Basque

Preparation time: 45 minutes
Cooking time: 1 hour
Difficulty: ★

**Serves 4**

| | |
|---|---|
| 1 | white onion |
| 1 | red onion |
| 1 clove | garlic |
| 2 | tomatoes |
| 7 tbsp/100 ml | olive oil |
| 2 | leeks |
| 2 cups/500 g | shrimp |
| 4 tbsp/60 ml | cognac |
| ²/₃ cups/150 ml | white wine |

| | |
|---|---|
| 5 tsp/25 g | cornstarch |
| 2 cups/500 g | sieved tomatoes (optional) |

| | |
|---|---|
| 1 lb 2 oz/500 g | mixed fish fillets (sole, hake, sea perch, scorpion fish etc.) |
| 2 cups/500 g | clams |
| | salt and pepper |

**For the fish stock:**

| | |
|---|---|
| 2¼ lb/1 kg | fish offcuts (heads, tails, bones, skin) |
| | the green of a leek |
| 1 | white onion |
| 3 | parsley stalks |

**For the garnish:**

| | |
|---|---|
| | parsley |
| | ground paprika (optional) |

Basque cuisine is dominated by the sea, and the range of recipes for fish and seafood is as extensive as it is varied. Because the Basques are very traditional, those throughout northern Spain still use the wonderful recipes devised by their ancestors. The Spanish name for this soup is *sopa de pezcado a la marinera*. It is a standard dish for fishermen's families, who always use whatever is caught. The soup is especially popular in winter.

You can use whatever fish is available. Emilio González Soto likes sole, because the flesh of this fish, which is at home on the sandy bottom of the Atlantic Ocean, is delicate and aromatic. He also likes to include scorpion fish—*rascasse* is a key ingredient of bouillabaisse—which is popular for its white, oily flesh.

Home-made fish stock is essential for the success of this dish. It is made from offcuts (heads, tails, bones, and skin), and is pure flavor. The stock, which also includes parsley, leek greens, and white onions, develops its typical aroma after being reduced and strained.

Basques love all kinds of shellfish, especially clams, usually plain or stuffed. Clams are gathered along the Atlantic coast, but they are also found in the Mediterranean, where another variety, the carpet shell—also known as the *clovisse*—hails from. Mussels can be used instead. The cognac emphasizes the typical aroma of this tasty soup.

You can also add sieved tomatoes—as we have done here—to enhance the color of the soup.

*Peel and thinly slice the white and red onions, and the garlic clove. Finely chop the tomatoes.*

*To make the fish stock, bring 8 cups (2 l) water to the boil with 1 lb 2 oz (500 g) fish offcuts, the green of a leek, a sliced white onion, and the parsley, then boil briskly for around 3 minutes.*

*Sauté in olive oil the finely sliced white of the leeks, tomatoes, onions, and garlic in olive oil. Simmer for 15 minutes. Prepare the shrimp, and put the heads in the pot. Add the remainder of the fish offcuts, stir, and simmer for 5 minutes.*

# Fish Soup

Add the cognac and wine, and stir. Strain this liquid through a sieve, add to the fish stock, then simmer for a further 30 minutes.

Blend the cornstarch with 7 tbsp (100 ml) water in a small bowl. Strain the soup through a sieve, then return to the heat and stir in the starch. Return to the boil, stirring continuously. Add the tomatoes to the bubbling soup.

Season with salt and pepper. Remove any foam with a skimmer. Add the shrimp, fish fillets, and clams, then bring to the boil. Remove from the heat, and leave to stand for 5 minutes. Pour into deep bowls. Garnish with parsley and ground paprika.

# Soup from

| | |
|---|---|
| Preparation time: | 40 minutes |
| Cooking time: | 50 minutes |
| Difficulty: | ★ |

**Serves 4**

| | |
|---|---|
| 1 | carrot |
| 1 | leek |
| 1 | onion |
| 7 tbsp/100 ml | olive oil |
| 4 large | shrimp |
| pinch | saffron |
| 4 tbsp/60 ml | Spanish brandy |
| 1 tsp | tomato concentrate |

| | |
|---|---|
| 4 tsp/20 g | rice |
| 1 lb 2 oz/500 g | angler fish |
| dash | pastis |
| | salt |

**For the fish stock:**

| | |
|---|---|
| 1 | leek |
| 1 | tomato |
| 1 | celery stalk |
| 2½ lb/1 kg | fish offcuts (heads, tails, bones, skin) |

**For the garnish (optional):**

| | |
|---|---|
| | chives |

This fish soup is named after the village of Villajoyosa, just a few miles from Alicante on the Mediterranean. The aromatic classic is extremely popular here, where culinary treasures from the sea are prized.

It is very easy to make. The main thing is the highly prized angler fish, whose fine, firm flesh is reminiscent of lobster. The soup was originally made with rockfish, which has a high iodine content that makes it very aromatic. Depending on what is available, you can also use sea perch instead of angler fish.

Over time, shrimp were added to the soup to further enhance it. This variety of seafood is the subject of endless discussions in Spain. Each coastal region claims to have the loveliest and best on the whole peninsula!

The addition of Spanish brandy from Jerez gives a special touch to this soup. The brandy, which carries a certificate of origin, may only be put in barrels in this region's bodegas (wineries).

According to legend, the brandy owes its existence to Dutch traders, who initially made sherry from a refined liqueur called *Hollanda*. One day, they ordered 500 barrels from a vintner in Jerez but were unable to pay him. The vintner poured the undelivered goods into old barrels that had contained aging sherry, and forgot about them. Some years later he found them again and sampled the contents: and Spanish brandy from Jerez was born.

Serve this delicious soup from Villajoyosa to favorite guests!

*To make the fish stock, roughly chop the leek, tomato, and celery, then put in a pot with the fish offcuts. Cover with water, and bring to the boil. Simmer for about 20 minutes, then strain and filter.*

*Finely chop the carrot, leek, and onions. Heat the olive oil in a pot, and sauté the vegetables. Add the shrimp in their shells, and season with salt. Crush the saffron threads.*

*Add the brandy, and continue simmering, stirring continuously.*

# Villajoyosa

Add the saffron, tomato concentrate, and the rice. Stir well.

Add the filtered fish stock, then simmer gently for about 20 minutes. Sieve the fish stock. Remove the shrimp from their shells, and cut the angler fish into pieces.

Check the seasoning and adjust if necessary. Return the angler fish and shrimp to the soup, and simmer for about 2 minutes. Add the pastis, then pour the soup into deep bowls. Garnish with chives before serving.

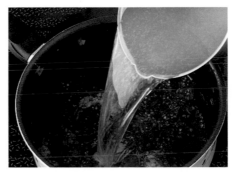

# Palm Sunday

| | |
|---|---|
| Preparation time: | *20 minutes* |
| Cooking time: | *30 minutes* |
| Difficulty: | ✳ |

**Serves 4**

| | |
|---|---|
| 2 | green bell peppers |
| 2 | red bell peppers |
| 16 stalks | green asparagus |
| 4 | tomatoes |

| | |
|---|---|
| 12 slices | white bread |
| | a little olive oil |
| 4 cloves | garlic |
| 8 cups/2 l | chicken stock |
| 4–5 | flat-leaf parsley stalks |
| | salt and pepper |

In spring, the inhabitants of Málaga love to prepare a selection of fine vegetables in clear stock. This dish is called *sopa de siete ramos*, which literally means "soup of the seven branches." According to history, the name reminds us of Easter week and the custom of consecrating palm or box branches on Palm Sunday.

Red and green bell peppers, tomatoes, garlic, and asparagus are the base for this delicious soup. Try to use wild asparagus if you can find it; according to Javier Valero, this is much better than the farmed variety. The green to lilac-colored stalks are very thin with an extremely characteristic aroma that is much prized in Spain.

However, green farmed asparagus is far more readily available, and can happily be used for this soup. In Spain it is grown primarily in Navarre, and harvested from April to June. The wooden stalk is removed before peeling. After blanching them, plunge the stalks in iced water so they retain their deep green color.

Pour boiling water over the tomatoes, then skin them and remove the seeds. Cut them into quarters; according to Javier Valero they then look like "petals."

The ingredients are all poached in chicken stock. You can make it from bouillon, but home-made stock is much tastier. To make your own, brown a chicken carcass with some soup vegetables (onion, cloves, carrots, bay leaf, celery, leek), then cover with water. Simmer for a good 90 minutes, then strain.

To serve, the vegetables are arranged on small plates with the croutons. The stock is served separately.

*Place the bell peppers on a foil-covered baking sheet, and broil for about 10 minutes. Using the tip of a sharp kitchen knife, remove the skin and cut the peppers into slices.*

*Wash the asparagus and pat dry. Peel from top to bottom, then blanch in boiling salted water for 5 minutes.*

*Place the tomatoes in a bowl, then pour over boiling water. As soon as the skin starts to lift, pour the water away and plunge the tomatoes into iced water. Peel with a small, sharp knife, remove the seeds, and cut the flesh into slices.*

# Soup

Cut the bread into cubes and sprinkle over a little olive oil. Place on a baking sheet and bake in a preheated oven for a few moments. Then rub each piece with a peeled garlic clove.

Bring the chicken stock to the boil. Add the asparagus, tomatoes, red and green bell peppers, and season with salt and pepper. Simmer for 5 minutes. Scoop the vegetables out of the stock with a skimmer.

Peel the remainder of the garlic and cut into thin slices. Sauté in hot olive oil, then add the parsley and pass through a sieve. Pour the stock into soup bowls. Serve the vegetables and croutons separately, and drizzle the flavored oil over the soup.

# Balearic

| | |
|---|---|
| Preparation time: | 30 minutes |
| Cooking time: | 1 hour 35 minutes |
| Difficulty: | ★ |

**Serves 4**

| | |
|---|---|
| 4 | thick carrots |
| 2 | white turnips |
| 2 | salsify roots |
| 1 | lettuce |
| 2 sprigs | thyme |

| | |
|---|---|
| 2 sprigs | rosemary |
| 2 sprigs | marjoram |
| 1 cup/250 g | fresh peas, shelled |
| 2 tbsp/30 ml | olive oil |
| 4 pinches | salt |
| 1 pinch | pepper |
| 2 pinches | sugar |
| 4 cups/1 l | fish stock (see pages 68 or 70 as an example) |
| 8 thin slices | baguette |

Javier Valero cannot imagine Spanish cuisine without soups, and that is evident from the menu in his restaurant "San Valero" in Neuilly, one of the best Spanish restaurants in France. On his frequent travels to his home, he gathers ideas and traditional recipes that are not known away from the Iberian Peninsula, as well as ideas for unusual combinations that guarantee truly cross-border culinary delights.

Herb soups are one of the everyday dishes that are often enhanced by fish and seafood such as langoustines, but also with meat, usually combined with delicious vegetables such as cabbage, and tomatoes. In the Balearics, the fine aroma of fresh marjoram is also added, which gives such an incomparable and characteristic flavor that the soup is as good cold as it is hot.

The inhabitants of the Balearics have always cooked well, and believe many of the plants that grow there to have healing or even magical properties. Marjoram, with its delicate stalks and bright green leaves, is one of them. Its aroma is reminiscent of mint, basil, and citrus fruits. Marjoram is used a great deal all over the Mediterranean, and its flavor goes just as well with strong meat dishes such as lamb and venison as it does with vegetable dishes, fish, and eggs.

One of the ingredients in this easily prepared, delicious soup is a simple lettuce. Instead of the usual white turnips, keep a lookout for small, tender, spring turnips.

Javier Valero recommends a white Galician Ribeiro or Rías Baixas with this herb soup.

*Peel, trim, and chop the carrots, turnips, and salsify.*

*Wash and slice the lettuce.*

*Put the carrots, turnips, salsify, and lettuce in a pot.*

# Herb Soup

Add the thyme, rosemary, marjoram leaves, and shelled peas. Cover with water. Add 2 tbsp (30 ml) olive oil. Season with salt, pepper, and sugar. Bring to the boil, then simmer gently for 1 hour until almost all of the liquid has evaporated.

Add the fish stock to the soup, then simmer for 25–30 minutes.

Fry the bread in olive oil until golden. Place two slices on the bottom of a soup bowl, then pour over the soup. Add a dash of olive oil, and serve immediately.

# Tomato Soup

| | |
|---|---|
| Preparation time: | *30 minutes* |
| Drain tomatoes: | *6 hours* |
| Cooking time: | *15 minutes* |
| Difficulty: | *✳* |

**Serves 4**

| | |
|---|---|
| 2¼ lb/1 kg | firm red tomatoes |
| 1 thick | scallion (spring onion) |
| 4–5 sprigs | basil |
| 1 clove | garlic |

| | |
|---|---|
| 2 slices | white bread |
| 7 tbsp/100 ml | olive oil |
| 1 | Cantaloupe melon |
| | a little sherry vinegar |
| pinch | sugar |
| 14 oz/400 g | fillet of red tuna |
| | salt and pepper |

As soon as the summer starts to warm up, the Valencians begin to think of gazpacho, the ice-cold Andalusian specialty. In order to remind his fellow citizens of their own culinary traditions, Oscar Torrijos had the idea of creating an original Valencian tomato soup.

Oscar Torrijos is of the opinion that tomatoes from Valencia (*Valencianos*) are the best variety for eating raw. The red fruits thrive in the open air and have a particularly strong aroma—as is often the case with old varieties. This variety is grown primarily around Valencia, in the Huerta, Spain's main fruit- and vegetable-growing region. *Valencianos* are a popular choice for use in salads and soups made of raw vegetables. They go wonderfully well with flavorsome dishes with tuna or seafood.

Our chef arranged broiled tuna medallions and golden-brown croutons on a plate. Tuna (*atún*, in Spanish) were caught along the Iberian coasts centuries ago by the Phoenicians and Romans. Today, Spanish fishing boats catch these huge fish in all of the world's oceans. On the Iberian Peninsula, red tuna is particularly prized for its higher fat content. Tuna is available fresh, canned, or dried (as in *mojama*).

The fish medallions are cooked the Spanish way: on a lightly oiled, red-hot steel griddle. The food is simply placed on the griddle and cooked without further ado. This method helps to retain the flavor, consistency, and most of the nutrients. Bonito, swordfish, and any other variety with firm, red flesh can be used instead of tuna.

*Halve the tomatoes and remove the seeds. Grate the tomatoes on a metal grater over a bowl, taking care not to grate the skin. Wrap the grated tomato in a cloth, then hang it up and leave to drain for about 6 hours.*

*Finely chop the scallion, basil, and garlic. Crush the garlic in a mortar and pestle, then set aside.*

*Remove the crusts from the bread, and cut the bread into small, evenly sized cubes. Heat 4 tbsp (60 ml) olive oil in a skillet, then fry the bread cubes for 3–4 minutes until golden yellow.*

# with Tuna

Halve the melon and remove the seeds. Scoop out small balls using a baller.

Combine the grated tomato with the onion, basil, and garlic, then season with salt and pepper. Combine well with the vinegar, sugar, and remainder of the olive oil.

Slice the tuna. Cut out circles with a cookie cutter, then broil on each side for about 5 minutes. Place two medallions on each plate, scattering the croutons in-between them. Pour tomato soup around the outside. Garnish with melon balls.

| | |
|---|---|
| Preparation time: | 10 minutes |
| Chilling time: | 20 minutes |
| Difficulty: | ★ |

**Serves 4**

| | |
|---|---|
| 3 cups/750 g | fresh strawberries |
| 1 | green bell pepper |
| 1 | red bell pepper |
| 1 | onion |
| 2 cloves | garlic |
| 2 tbsp/30 g | confectioner's sugar |

| | |
|---|---|
| ³/₄ cup/200 ml | olive oil |
| 6½ tbsp/100 ml | sherry vinegar |
| 1 tsp | salt |
| 1 tsp | pepper |

**For the garnish (optional):**

chopped red bell pepper
chopped green bell
  pepper
croutons

José Luis Tarín Fernández's brightly colored, nutritious and refreshing strawberry soup is proof of the creativity of modern Spanish cuisine. Much is reminiscent of Andalusian gazpacho, the main difference being that this recipe uses sweetly aromatic strawberries instead of tomatoes. The soup is so original that no other fruit can be used as a substitute for the strawberries unless you want something slightly more acidic, in which case add a handful of raspberries.

To make the soup nice and mild, use very ripe summer strawberries with a firm flesh. Choose large, fully ripe specimens with no marks. Strawberries are very delicate and must be handled with care. Wash them quickly under running cold water, then leave them to drain.

Bell peppers are a firm fixture in Spanish cuisine, and can be combined with any number of sauces. Whether a slightly

acid green or a mild red bell pepper, the main thing is that the peppers are bright in color with a smooth, shiny skin. The thin white pith and seeds are removed because they are indigestible. The sweet aroma of the red bell pepper can overpower the delicate flavor of the strawberries. Chef therefore adds a little sherry vinegar for its slight tartness. Vinegar made from sherry is very spicy. It is also quite viscous, and does not readily dissolve. Add the required amount to the soup in several small amounts and stir well. If you do not happen to have any sherry vinegar to hand, use a few drops of balsamic.

The strawberry soup is puréed in the blender, then passed through a sieve. Chill in the refrigerator for a few minutes before serving. Croutons go well with this dish.

*Trim the strawberries. Carefully remove the stalks and leaves without damaging the fruits. Wash the strawberries under running cold water, then place in a sieve to drain. Cut into quarters.*

*Wash the bell peppers and pat them dry, then cut in half lengthwise. Remove the pith and seeds. Cut the peppers into quarters, then cut these into chunks 1 in (3 cm) in length. Do the same with the peeled onion. Peel and halve the garlic.*

*Place the bell peppers, onion, garlic, and strawberries in the blender, then add the salt, pepper, and sugar. Purée carefully for 2–3 minutes until you have a velvety-smooth, well-blended mixture.*

# Strawberry Soup

Remove the lid from the blender and pour in half the olive oil. Run the machine again at high speed, then add the remainder of the olive oil and run for a further 2–3 minutes.

Place a sieve over a bowl. Ladle the soup into it in several portions, and pass through the sieve using the ladle to squeeze as much liquid as possible out of the flesh.

Add the vinegar, and stir in well until it has completely dissolved. Check the soup, adding more seasoning if required, then chill for 20 minutes. Serve very cold but not icy. Garnish with diced bell peppers, and croutons.

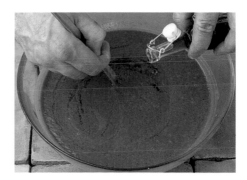

# Cold Almond Soup

Preparation time: 30 minutes
Cooking time: 10 minutes
Difficulty: ★

**Serves 4**

| | |
|---|---|
| 4 oz/100 g | grapes |
| 1½ cups/350 ml | virgin olive oil |
| 1½ cups/350 g | skinned almonds |

| | |
|---|---|
| ½ | day-old baguette |
| 1 clove | garlic |
| 5 tbsp/80 ml | sherry vinegar |
| | salt and pepper |

**For the garnish:**

| | |
|---|---|
| 4 | chive stalks |

There is an old Spanish tradition of enhancing everyday meals with delicious soups. Soups are essential as an appetizer or the main part of a light evening meal. Fresh vegetables are usually used for these simple, delicate soups, so this delightful cold almond soup—a specialty from Málaga—is something of an exception. It is very easy to make, but its charm lies in the quality of the ingredients; the utmost care is taken when choosing them.

The process starts with the almonds. They are used dried rather than harvested fresh. Spain's almond trees flower in the spring, so the almonds used are usually from domestic trees. The growing region extends from Tarragona to Valencia and Málaga, but there are also plantations in Granada and Almería, and on the Canary Islands. There are many different varieties of almonds, all of different shapes, which range from long and slender to heart-shaped. These versatile nuts are served with an aperitif or as a satisfying snack, and are used in countless baked goods, candies, and desserts. They used to be an important source of protein: a single almond contains 45 percent fat, plenty of iron, calcium, phosphorus, and vitamin B.

The olive oil used should have an acid content of 0.2 to 0.4 degrees.

The soup is passed through a sieve to make it nice and smooth. Traditionally it is served with bread, grapes, and thin slices of sweet melon. Essentially a simple soup, it looks particularly appealing if served in stemmed glasses.

*Remove the grapes from the stalks. Carefully cut them in half with a sharp knife, and remove the seeds.*

*Heat 4 tbsp (60 ml) of olive oil and sauté the blanched almonds until golden.*

*Cut the crusts off the baguette, and cut the bread into strips, then into 1 in (3 cm) squares.*

# from Málaga

Peel the garlic, and remove the core. Purée in the blender, together with the almonds.

Add the diced bread and continue blending, gradually adding the vinegar and the remainder of the olive oil. When the mixture is smooth, add 4 cups (1 l) of water, then season with salt and pepper.

Pour the almond soup into soup bowls or stemmed glasses. Garnish with grapes and chopped chives.

Fish &
Seafood

# Eels

| | |
|---|---|
| Preparation time: | *45 minutes* |
| Cooking time: | *1 hour 15 minutes* |
| Difficulty: | ★★ |

**Serves 4**

| | |
|---|---|
| 8 oz/200 g | potatoes |
| 2¼ lb/1 kg | large eels |
| 4–5 | parsley stalks |
| 7 tbsp/100 ml | olive oil |

| | |
|---|---|
| 3 cloves | garlic |
| 1 | dried red chile |
| 1 tsp | mild ground paprika |
| | salt and pepper |

**For the picada (spicy paste):**

| | |
|---|---|
| 20 | almonds, skinned |
| 2 tbsp/30 ml | olive oil |
| 2 | parsley stalks |
| ½ clove | garlic |

After paella, eels with *salsa all i pebre* (garlic and paprika sauce) is the second best-known specialty from Valencia. However, because the preparation requires the skill of an experienced chef, it is only ever found on menus at the best restaurants near the coast of Albufera.

The preparations for eels with *salsa al i pebre* usually begin with the sauce. Braise the potatoes, paprika, and eels together to make a kind of ragout. Oscar Torrijos cooks each one of the main ingredients separately, and combines them just before serving. This way each ingredient retains its consistency, color, and flavor.

Eel is extremely popular in Spain. Over the course of its life this unusual fish migrates from saltwater to freshwater, from sea to river, returning to its spawning ground thousands of miles from Europe in the Sargasso Sea between Florida and the Azores in the south-west Atlantic.

The tiny elvers are then transported by the Gulf Stream to Europe, where they swim upriver.

Oscar Torrijos cuts the potatoes into ½ in (1.2 cm) thick slices, and cuts evenly sized circles out of the slices. He boils the circles in salted water, to which he adds a little olive oil to prevent them from falling apart.

If the sauce separates during preparation—if the oil fails to combine with the firm ingredients—then simply blend everything together to make a smooth purée.

Oscar Torrijos arranges the eel fillets and potatoes on plates, and serves the sauce separately. We do things slightly differently in this recipe by putting a little sauce on the plates. You can also dress the potatoes in olive oil and sliced almonds, thinly sliced chile, pine nuts, and ground paprika.

*Peel and slice the potatoes, then boil in salted water for 20 minutes. To make the picada, fry the almonds for 5 minutes in a skillet in olive oil. Chop the parsley. Peel the garlic, and crush everything in a mortar.*

*Cut the eel into 4 in (10 cm) pieces, and remove the insides. Wash under running cold water, then pat dry, and remove the fillets along the middle bone. Skin the fillets, reserving the bones. Place the fillets on a plate.*

*Using a pair of tweezers, remove all the bones from the fish. Season the fillets with salt and pepper, and sprinkle with chopped parsley.*

# from Valencia

Heat the olive oil in a pot, then fry the eel bones and chopped garlic over a high heat for 5 minutes. Cover with water, and simmer the stock for about 30 minutes. Sieve and filter.

Quickly fry the dried chile in oil in another pot. Add the picada, ground paprika, and finally the fish stock, then simmer for 20 minutes—and you have your Salsa al i pebre.

Heat a little oil in a large non-stick skillet, and fry the eel fillets over a high heat for 10 minutes. Serve the pieces of eel with the sliced potatoes and the sauce.

# Stockfish with

| | |
|---|---|
| Preparation time: | 30 minutes |
| Soaking time for | |
| garbanzo beans | |
| and stockfish: | 24 hours |
| Cooking time: | 1 hour 15 minutes |
| Difficulty: | ★★ |

**Serves 4**

| | |
|---|---|
| 2¼ lb/1 kg | stockfish |
| 1 lb 2 oz/500 g | garbanzo beans (chickpeas) |
| ½ | onion, finely chopped |
| 8 tbsp/120 ml | olive oil |

| | |
|---|---|
| 3½ tbsp/50 g | flour |
| 1 tsp | mild ground paprika |
| 8 oz/200 g | fresh spinach |
| 2 | eggs |
| 2 slices | bread |
| 4 tbsp/60 ml | sunflower oil |
| 2 cloves | garlic |

**For the bouquet garni:**

| | |
|---|---|
| | green of 1 leek |
| 1 | thyme stalk |
| 2 | bay leaves |

In Spain, people like to eat stockfish with garbanzo beans in the *Semana Santa* (the week before Easter), which is treated liked a public festival. Every day there are long pilgrimages in the towns. Believers carry heavy statues of saints, and draw lavishly decorated wagons through the streets. After the procession, family and friends meet up and share their favorite dishes. These include stockfish in various guises, especially around Córdoba and Jaén in Andalusia.

Cod has been fished in all the world's cold oceans for centuries. It is dried to make stockfish; strictly speaking, the fish that is dried and preserved with salt is called "klipfish." In bygone days, stockfish used to be prepared in many different ways in rural Spain; most people could afford this inexpensive, extremely long-lasting fish.

Stockfish can be bought in advance, but should be kept in a sealed container in the refrigerator.

The fish is soaked in cold water a day before it is needed to make it nice and tender. The water needs to be changed several times during the 24-hour soaking period. The tail of the fish is cut off and added to the cooking liquid for the garbanzo beans. Depending on the size and hardness of the garbanzo beans, they will take about 50 minutes to cook on the hob, but only about 10 in a pressure cooker. Keep scooping off the froth from the top as they cook.

Some chefs enhance the dish with bread that has been coated in parsley and garlic to make the dish more nutritious. As well as the various vegetables, fried potatoes can also be served as an accompaniment.

*Soak the pieces of stockfish and garbanzo beans overnight. Put a pot of water on to boil with the stockfish tail, the garbanzo beans, and the bouquet garni. Bring to the boil and simmer for about 50 minutes.*

*Cook the onion in 4 tbsp (60 ml) of olive oil in a small pot until transparent, but do not let it turn brown. Add the flour and ground paprika with a little water, and sweat, stirring briskly.*

*Drain the garbanzo beans as soon as they are just firm to the bite. Reserve the cooking liquid, adding some to the onion mixture to make a slightly thick flour-based sauce. Add the garbanzo beans.*

# Garbanzo Beans

Trim and wash the spinach. Simmer in 4 tbsp (60 ml) of olive oil in a large skillet until the leaves collapse. Boil the eggs for 10 minutes until hard, then peel and remove the yolks. Chop the whites.

Fry the slices of bread in sunflower oil in a skillet. Peel and crush the garlic in a mortar with the egg yolks and fried bread until smooth.

Add the spinach, bread-and-egg paste, chopped egg whites, and the pieces of stockfish to the garbanzo beans. Boil vigorously for 5 minutes.

# Monkfish

Preparation time: 45 minutes
Cooking time: 30 minutes
Difficulty: ★

**Serves 4**

| | |
|---|---|
| 1 lb 14 oz/800 g | monkfish |
| 1 lb 2 oz/500 g | fresh peas |
| 4 | shrimps |
| 8 | clams |
| | a little olive oil |
| 4 stalks | white asparagus (canned) |
| | salt |

**For the fish stock:**

| | |
|---|---|
| 1 | leek |
| 2 | parsley stalks |

| | |
|---|---|
| ½ | white onion, chopped |
| 2¼ lb/1 kg | fish offcuts (heads, tails, bones, skin) |

**For the green sauce:**

| | |
|---|---|
| 1 bunch | flat-leaf parsley |
| 2 cloves | garlic |
| 7 tbsp/100 ml | olive oil |
| ⅞ cup/100 g | flour |
| | salt and white pepper |

**For the batter:**

| | |
|---|---|
| 2 | eggs |
| ¼ cup/25 g | flour |
| ⅔ cup/150 ml | olive oil |
| | salt |

**For the garnish (optional):**

| | |
|---|---|
| | dried red chile |

Emilio González Soto grew up in the family restaurant. Over the years he learned his craft from his father, who was known affectionately as *Currito*—"Little one"—by one and all. The son also inherited his father's passion for cooking. Today, Emilio continues the family tradition of lovingly prepared Basque specialties in Santurce, about 10 miles (15 km) from Bilbao.

Monkfish Currito-style is a delightful homage to Emilio's father, to whom the young chef owes much. Although easy to prepare, the dish is absolutely delicious, not least because of the typical green sauce, which is often served with monkfish in the Basque Country.

Serving this sauce with monkfish is a brilliant idea. The fish is greatly prized for its firm, white flesh—the consistency and aroma of which are similar to lobster. Monkfish can be cooked almost any way you like. If you can't get this fish, then cod is a good substitute for this recipe.

The spicy green sauce is not just popular in the Basque Country; it is an essential accompaniment to many dishes, and goes very well with fish. It consists of parsley, garlic, flour, olive oil, salt, and white pepper, and it is a Mediterranean specialty.

The main ingredient is flat-leaf parsley; the Spanish adore its characteristic aroma. The herb has the advantage of being available all year round, but it should be used fresh, with dark-green leaves and firm stalks. Emilio González Soto suggests trying fresh spinach as an alternative.

*To make the fish stock, boil 4 cups (1 l) water, and add the finely chopped leek, parsley, and fish offcuts. Cover with a lid, and simmer gently for about 20 minutes.*

*For the green sauce, roughly chop the parsley, then peel and crush the garlic. Heat the olive oil in a pot. Sauté the garlic, parsley, and flour. Stir. Strain the fish stock, and combine with the flour mixture, stirring continuously. Cook for 3 minutes, then season with salt and pepper.*

*Cut the monkfish into evenly sized pieces. Shell the peas, then boil in salted water for 6–8 minutes. Set aside.*

# Currito-Style

To make the batter, break the eggs into a bowl and whisk them. Season the monkfish pieces with salt, then coat them in flour, and dip them in the egg. Deep-fry in olive oil until golden.

Shell the shrimp and devein them (that is, remove the dark vein from the back of the shrimp). Place in the green sauce, together with the clams and monkfish pieces, then drizzle over a little olive oil. Simmer gently.

When the clams open, add the peas and asparagus, then simmer for 2 minutes. Arrange on plates. Garnish with slices of dried chile.

# Fish Stew

| | |
|---|---|
| Preparation time: | 40 minutes |
| Cooking time: | 40 minutes |
| Difficulty: | ★★ |

**Serves 6**

| | |
|---|---|
| 3 | tomatoes |
| 2 | potatoes |
| 2 | onions |
| 4 cloves | garlic |
| 2 | green bell peppers |

| | |
|---|---|
| 2 | red bell peppers |
| 2 cups/500 ml | olive oil |
| 6½ tbsp/100 g | ground almonds |
| | saffron threads |
| 2 tbsp/30 ml | dry white wine |
| 2¼ lb/1 kg | prepared clams |
| 1⅔ cups/400 g | thin Spanish noodles (fideos) |
| 8 cups/2 l | fish stock (see the previous recipe) |
| | salt and pepper |

Stews made of vegetables, seafood, and thin noodles are prepared by many fishing families along the coasts of Spain. Noodles often used to be a substitute for rice when none was available.

The vegetables for this colorful dish—which melts on the tongue—are cut into tiny pieces called *brunoises*. The potatoes are first cut into thin strips, then diced. The bell peppers are cut in half lengthwise to remove the seeds and pith, then the strips are diced. The tomatoes are dipped in boiling water, skinned and the seeds removed before being cut into eighths and chopped. The vegetables are all cooked over a low heat for 3 to 4 minutes without browning, so they need to be watched constantly. The tomatoes are added at the end. For this recipe, the Spanish use a flat paella dish with two handles that distributes the heat evenly.

The clams need to be washed thoroughly before using to remove all traces of sand. Dispose of any clams that are open. When the vegetables are cooked and you have added the almond paste, add the clams and cook at high heat; they will open very quickly.

The main ingredient in this dish is thin noodles known as *fideos*, which can be thick or thin, straight or curvy. They are added uncooked to the vegetables and shellfish, then everything is cooked—like paella—in hot oil. The fish stock enhances the aroma.

*Aiolo*—a sauce made of garlic, salt, egg yolks, and oil—goes extremely well with this dish, as does a sauce made of olive oil, flat-leaf parsley, and chives.

*Pour boiling water over the tomatoes and skin them. Wash and/or peel the potatoes, onions, garlic, and bell peppers. Cut the bell peppers in half, and remove the pith and seeds. Finely dice the bell peppers, tomatoes, and potatoes. Finely chop the onions and garlic.*

*Heat 1⅔ cups (400 ml) olive oil in a paella pan, and sauté the garlic and onions over a low heat for 3–4 minutes. Add the chopped potato and bell peppers, then simmer for 10 minutes. Add the tomatoes, then season with salt and pepper, and simmer for a further 2–3 minutes.*

*Crush the almonds in a mortar together with 7 tbsp (100 ml) olive oil, the saffron threads, salt, and pepper, then blend in the white wine.*

# with Thin Noodles

Add spoonfuls of this paste to the vegetables.

Add the clams to the vegetables, and cook over a high heat for 1–2 minutes.

Add the noodles. Combine well, and simmer gently for 2 minutes. Pour over the fish stock, and continue simmering gently for 10–15 minutes. Serve very hot.

# Squid

Preparation time: 20 minutes
Cooking time: 25 minutes
Difficulty: ✷

**Serves 4**

| | |
|---|---|
| 1 lb 2 oz/500 g | small squid |
| 8 tbsp/120 ml | olive oil |
| 2 cloves | garlic |

| | |
|---|---|
| 1 | large onion |
| ⅛ cup/15 g | flour |
| pinch | mild ground paprika |
| 2 lb/900 g | fresh fava beans |
| | (broad beans) |
| | salt |

Squid with fava beans is a favorite summer dish of the inhabitants of Granada. The prettily colored combination of squid and tender beans is served in an onion sauce. The ground paprika adds just the right flavour.

Small squid are the preferred choice for this recipe; they are called *chocos* in Andalusia, and *pota* or *jibia* elsewhere. They are smaller than *chipirones* (calamaries), and are caught young, so they are much more tender than older specimens. They must not be cooked for long, as they can become tough during cooking. At home all over the Mediterranean, squid are a member of the cephalopod family. The oval, slightly flat, sack-like body is yellow to beige in color, with black stripes and two tiny fins. There are ten tentacles around the mouth opening and eyes: eight short ones, and two that are much longer.

After cleaning them and removing the cuttlebone, wash the squid well under running water. José-Ignacio Herráiz rubs them well between his fingers to remove all traces of skin, sand, and dirt.

To make this dish, sweat the garlic and onions over a low heat; they should be transparent without turning brown. Then do the same to the pieces of squid, and add the fava beans at the end. 2¼ lb (1 kg) of fava bean pods produces just under 1 lb (400 g) of shelled beans. Make sure that the pods are of average size, bright green, and have no black spots on them. To shell them, squeeze the pointed end of the pod between your fingers until it bursts open, then separate them along the "thread." Remove the skin and the tiny sprouts from the beans. Once prepared, the beans don't take long to cook.

Cut the heads off the squid and cut out the cuttlebone. Clean the fish, wash under running water, and skin them. Turn the "mantles" inside out, and wash thoroughly inside and out. Cut the flesh into cubes. Shell and skin the beans.

Heat 4 tbsp (60 ml) of olive oil in a skillet until very hot, and fry the chopped squid for 3–4 minutes until golden yellow.

Peel and chop the garlic and onions. Heat 4 tbsp (60 ml) of olive oil in a skillet. Quickly fry the garlic. Add the onions, and cook for 5 minutes until transparent. Sprinkle over the flour, ground paprika, and salt, then cook for 2–3 minutes, stirring continuously.

# with Beans

Add the chopped squid, and continue cooking over a high heat, still stirring.

Cover the contents of the skillet with water, and continue cooking for 3–4 minutes.

Add the beans to the skillet, and stir well. Cook for a further 5 minutes until the beans are still just firm to the bite. Serve very hot.

# Turbot Fillets

Preparation time: 35 minutes
Cooking time: 8 minutes
Difficulty: ★

**Serves 4**

| | |
|---|---|
| 3¼ lb/1.5 kg | turbot |
| 8 tbsp/120 ml | olive oil |
| 12 oz/300 g | chanterelles |
| 2 cloves | garlic |
| ½ bunch | parsley |
| 1 bunch | chives |
| | salt |

Galicia is situated on the north-west coast of Spain, a region shaped by the forces of nature into a landscape that is as impressive as it is wild. The Galicians have been seafarers since time immemorial, and know well how to make full use of the ocean's bounty. Today, the Galician fishing fleet is at home on every one of the planet's oceans. Spain's biggest fishing harbor is in Vigo. The town, which is also known as "Barcelona on the Atlantic Coast," is so oriented to fish and fishing that the daily prices for the main fish and seafood varieties are published in the local newspaper, the *Faro de Vigo*.

The Galicians are considered gourmets, and never miss an opportunity to enjoy the excellent fish and seafood that is available on their doorstep. Turbot is one of the most popular of the 80-plus varieties caught here.

In this recipe, María Lourdes Fernández-Estevez combines the wonderful white fish with tasty chanterelles. The recipe requires very little effort, and cooks in minutes. Turbot, which is a native of the Atlantic, has a very tender, aromatic flesh, and is considered a particularly high-quality fish.

Just outside the Galician town of Lira-Carnota is a fish farm that produces over 600 tons of farmed turbot every year. It has to be said, though, that they are not quite as tasty as their cousins from the ocean. Substitute sole, sea bass, or sea perch, depending on what is available.

The chanterelles add a fruity-peppery aroma to the dish. These forest mushrooms are recognizable by their strong orange color and unusual shape. If chanterelles are not available, use honey mushrooms instead.

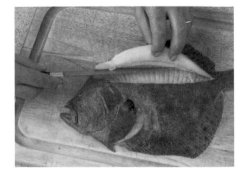

Fillet the turbot, and season the fillets with salt. Measure 2 tbsp (30 ml) of olive oil into a dish, and place the fillets on top.

Briefly cook the fillets under the broiler without adding any additional oil. Turn them over with a spatula.

Place the fillets in an ovenproof dish, then finish cooking in the oven (320 °F/160 °C) for about 3 minutes.

# with Chanterelles

Trim the chanterelles, then wash under running water. Wash and finely chop the parsley. Peel and crush the garlic. Heat 2 tbsp (30 ml) of olive oil in a skillet. Sweat the parsley and garlic, then season with salt. Add the chanterelles. Cook for about 3 minutes.

Wash and finely chop the chives.

In a blender, combine the chives with the remainder of the olive oil. Arrange the turbot fillets and chanterelles on plates, then drizzle over the chive sauce.

# Lobster with

Preparation time: 1 hour
Cooking time: 2 hours
Difficulty: ★★★

**Serves 4**

| | |
|---|---|
| 3¼ lb/1.5 kg | lobster |
| ⅔ cup/150 ml | olive oil |
| 1 lb 2 oz/500 g | rockfish (sea perch, scorpion fish, etc.) |
| 4 oz/100 g each | mushrooms, carrots, leeks, zucchini |
| 1 | tomato |
| 1 | red bell pepper |
| 2 oz/50 g | thin noodles |
| | salt |

**For the roast vegetables:**

| | |
|---|---|
| 4 oz/100 g | onions |
| 8 oz/200 g | leeks |

| | |
|---|---|
| 8 oz/200 g | carrots |
| 2 cloves | garlic |

**For the bouquet garni:**

| | |
|---|---|
| 2 sprigs | thyme |
| 3–4 sprigs | parsley |
| 1 | bay leaf |

**For the herb mayonnaise:**

| | |
|---|---|
| 2 | eggs |
| ⅔ cup/150 ml | olive oil |
| ⅔ cup/150 ml | groundnut oil |
| 1 | lemon |
| 1 tbsp each | dill, chives, chervil |
| | salt |

According to the story, one day the fishermen of Gandia were out on their boat and realized they had run out of rice for their paella. Necessity being the mother of invention, they used some leftover thin noodles—and the results were so good they passed on the recipe. Today, this "leftover" dish is known as *fideuà*, and has become a firm fixture on menus in Valencia and Gandia. There is even an annual international competition!

Oscar Torrijos transforms this popular dish into a culinary experience that leaves nothing to be desired: a feast for every one of the senses. The juicy pieces of lobster lie on nests of thin noodles and vegetables cooked in a stock of crustaceans and iodine-rich fish. The latter are usually used as a garnish for the noodles, and are cooked slowly in a spicy stock. Small scorpion fish, rainbow wrasse and tiny, boney red mullet add flavor and consistency to the stock.

Lobster is the crowning glory on the noodle nests. Formerly in abundance in Spanish waters, crustaceans now have to be imported. Lobster, which is as tender as it is expensive, can easily be replaced by langoustine, mantis shrimps or scampi. Oscar Torrijos starts by sautéing the garlic to add flavor to the fish stock from the beginning. He then adds the lobster head, and fries it until it is bright red and aromatic. Next, he adds the vegetables, followed by the fish and a bouquet garni.

Before he puts the claws in the pan he breaks them open with a meat tenderizer. The fried lobster pieces are plunged into cold water, which ends the cooking process abruptly, enabling you to remove the meat without burning your fingers. Then it takes just 10 minutes to finish cooking the lobster in the stock.

*Cook the lobster in boiling water. Remove the head, and cut the tail in half lengthwise. Heat 6½ tbsp (100 ml) olive oil in a pot. Fry the lobster head and the finely chopped roast vegetables for 10 minutes. Add the finely chopped rockfish, bouquet garni, 8 cups (2 l) water, and cook for 1 hour.*

*Trim and wash the onions, then cut them into thin slices. Thinly slice the carrots, leeks, and zucchini. Finely chop the tomato and bell pepper.*

*Heat a little oil in a pot until very hot. Fry the salted lobster tail and claws over a high heat for 5 minutes until they turn red, turning them once. Plunge into cold water. Remove the meat from the shells, and set aside.*

# Thin Noodles

Heat the remainder of the oil in a skillet. Fry the sliced mushrooms, chopped bell pepper, and tomato for 10 minutes until the liquid has evaporated. Season with salt, then add the noodles and continue cooking for 5 minutes, stirring continuously.

Add the zucchini, leek, and carrot strips. Season with salt, and cook for a further 10–15 minutes, stirring continuously. Add ³/₄ cup (200 ml) of the fish stock and lobster meat. Simmer for a further 10 minutes, adding a little more of the stock.

Make the herb mayonnaise. Place round molds on a serving dish and fill with the noodle and vegetable mix, then garnish with the lobster meat. Remove the molds. Serve the noodles and lobster with the herb mayonnaise.

# Angler Fish

Preparation time:    40 minutes
Cooking time:        50 minutes
Difficulty:          ✻

**Serves 4**

| | |
|---|---|
| 2¼ lb/1 kg | angler fish |
| 1²/₃ cups/400 ml | olive oil |
| 1¾ lb/800 g | potatoes |
| ⁷/₈ cup/100 g | flour |
| ¾ cup/200 ml | fish stock |
| 3 cloves | garlic |
| 2 | eggs |
| | salt |

Pep Masiques likes to use his mother's recipe for angler fish. Fish medallions and slices of potato are covered in *alioli*—a sauce made of garlic, salt, egg yolks, and oil—and then baked in the oven.

Angler fish, or sea-devil—*rape* in Castilian—is a deep-sea fish that prefers a sandy sea bottom near the coast. Rather than scales, it has a firm skin that is hard to remove. To fillet the fish, use a knife to cut along the middle bone. Then separate the skin from the head to the tail with your hands. Now put the fish on its back, and repeat on the abdominal side. Cut the fish into medallions, and fry them quickly in olive oil. Finish cooking the medallions in the oven. Cook the bones, skin, and fins together with some aromatic vegetables (carrots, celery, leeks) and seasoning to make a delicious home-made fish stock that can be used to cook the fish.

Peel and slice the potatoes, then put them in cold water to stop them from turning brown. Drain them before cooking, and pat them dry, then brown them in a very hot skillet. The skillet should be large enough for the potatoes to spread out and cook evenly.

The sauce adds spice and color to the dish. *Alioli*, known as *all i oli* in Catalan, means "garlic and oil." Originally it was made by crushing garlic in a mortar with a pinch of salt, and then gradually adding oil. Today, most recipes also include egg yolk. The eggs should not be too cold, otherwise the sauce will not thicken properly. So remember to take them out of the refrigerator in advance. You can whisk the sauce with a balloon whisk or an electric stick blender. If it is too thick, just add a few drops of water to make it smooth and thin, and it will coat the fish pieces evenly.

*Skin the angler fish and cut off the fins. Cut the meat into medallions and coat in flour. Fry in olive oil for 5 minutes, then set aside.*

*Heat some more olive oil in the same skillet. Cook the peeled, sliced potatoes for 10 minutes at high heat.*

*Pour over the fish stock, and cook for 25 minutes.*

# with Alioli

Place the cooked potatoes in a clay pot, then pour over the stock and season with salt. Arrange the fish pieces on top.

Peel and slice the garlic. Put in a bowl with salt and 2 egg yolks, and blend, gradually adding the oil, until you have a nice, velvety sauce.

Spoon the sauce over the fish pieces, then broil in a preheated oven for 10 minutes until golden. Serve in the clay dish.

# Hake with

Preparation time: 20 minutes
Cooking time: 30 minutes
Difficulty: ★

**Serves 4**

| | |
|---|---|
| 6½ tbsp/100 g | filberts (hazelnuts) |
| 1 lb 6 oz/600 g | hake |
| 1½ cup/150 g | flour |
| 7 tbsp/100 ml | olive oil |

| | |
|---|---|
| 4 cloves | garlic |
| 2 cups/500 ml | fish stock (see pages 68 or 70 as an example) |
| 1 bunch | fresh parsley |
| 4–5 | chive stalks |
| | salt and pepper |

This specialty from Madrid combines hake and filberts. It is available in numerous restaurants in the Spanish capital. The slices of fish are coated in flour, then fried with garlic and filberts, and finished off in a fish stock.

Hake is one of the most popular types of fish of the Spanish coast. The long, rounded body is gray along the back with golden spots, and white on the belly. The fish grows to a length of between 12 inches and 3 feet (30–100 cm). It has a large mouth full of sharp teeth but no beard threads, two back fins, and one rear fin. The meat contains just a few bones, which are easily removed. The Spanish call this fish *merluza*. In winter, predatory hake gather in large groups off the coast to gorge themselves on vast shoals of sardines. They spend the days in deep waters, coming to the surface at night to hunt. They eat quickly, and large amounts, so they soon become heavy and slow, which makes it easier for fishermen to catch them. Hake are also caught off the Basque coast. The quality is very much prized—but they are priced accordingly, so they are usually only found on menus in the best restaurants. For this recipe, you can substitute angler fish, perch or turbot if you like.

Filberts are cousins to hazelnuts, which can be used instead. If the filberts for the sauce are very dry, they can be difficult to skin. You may find it easier to scrape them with a sharp knife.

After adding the stock, the thickness of the fish slices will determine the remainder of the cooking time. The sauce is quite thin at the end of the cooking time; add a little flour to make it thicker if you like.

*Blanch the filberts in boiling water, then skin and roughly chop them. Cut the fish into slices, and season with salt and pepper. Peel and thinly slice the garlic.*

*Pour the flour onto a plate, and coat the fish on both sides until completely covered.*

*Heat the olive oil in a skillet. Fry the garlic and filberts for 3 minutes until golden, then push them to the side of the skillet.*

# Filbert Sauce

Fry the hake for about 5 minutes on each side in the same oil.

Add the fish stock, bring to the boil, and simmer for 15 minutes.

Sprinkle chopped parsley and chives over the fish. Pour over a little stock from the skillet, and serve immediately.

# Hake with

| | |
|---|---|
| Preparation time: | 30 minutes |
| Cooking time: | 45 minutes |
| Difficulty: | ★ |

**Serves 4**

| | |
|---|---|
| 2¼ lb/1 kg | hake |
| 2 | onions |
| 1 clove | garlic |
| 7 tbsp/100 ml | olive oil |

| | |
|---|---|
| 2 | sour oranges |
| 8 oz/200 g | light farmhouse bread |
| | salt |

**For the bouquet garni:**

| | |
|---|---|
| | green of 1 leek |
| 2 | bay leaves |
| 4–5 sprigs | parsley |

**For the garnish:**

| | |
|---|---|
| 1–2 | sweet oranges |

Hake with *caldillo de perro*—literally, "dog sauce"—is a specialty of the Cádiz region. Our chef steams the fish in an unusual sauce of garlic, onions, and bread soaked in orange juice, which adds a fruity-sour touch to the dish. It is common in Andalusia to thicken sauces and soups with bread, whereas flour or cornstarch are used elsewhere in Spain.

Hake, or *merluza*, is a typically Spanish fish. It is abundant in the waters of the Iberian Peninsula. It can also be replaced by whiting (*merlan*), which is cheaper and therefore often preferred by many Spanish families.

You can buy the fish whole (in which case you can use the head and bones for a fish stock) or in ready-to-use slices. In the latter case ask the fishmonger for the offcuts. Season your fish stock with a bouquet garni, carrots, and a clove-covered onion. Pour on enough of the stock to cover the fish. However, make sure the stock is not too hot, as otherwise the fish could disintegrate.

Covered with a lid, the cooking time is about 4 minutes per side. If your pot is high enough to cover the slices completely, you do not need to turn them.

It is difficult to find the sour oranges required for the recipe outside Spain. Use the juice from ordinary oranges with a little lemon juice instead. You could also put a small bowl with a combination of these juices on the table if you and your guests like a really sour taste.

*Clean the fish and cut diagonally into slices. To make the stock, put the head and bones in a pot of hot water, add 1 chopped onion and the bouquet garni, then cook for 30 minutes.*

*Brown the chopped garlic in olive oil in a skillet, then add the second chopped onion and cook.*

*Meanwhile, halve the sour oranges, and squeeze out the juice. Cut the bread into slices and remove the crust. Tear the remainder into chunks, place in the orange juice, and squash with a fork.*

# Caldillo de Perro

Season the fish with salt, and place in the skillet with the garlic and onions.

Now add the soaked bread, and cook over a high heat for 1–2 minutes.

Sieve the fish stock, and use a ladle to add to the fish. Cover with a lid, then simmer for about 8 minutes. Garnish with freshly peeled orange quarters if desired.

# Stockfish

| | |
|---|---|
| Preparation time: | 30 minutes |
| Soaking the stockfish: | 48 hours |
| Cooking time: | 1 hour |
| Difficulty: | ★ |

**Serves 4**

| | |
|---|---|
| 1¾ lb/800 g | stockfish |
| 1¼ cups/300 ml | olive oil |
| 2 | red bell peppers |

| | |
|---|---|
| 2 | onions |
| 3 cloves | garlic |
| 2 | ripe tomatoes, cut into quarters |
| 3 | eggplants |
| 1½ cups/150 g | flour |
| | salt |

Through this recipe the chef, Pep Masiques, has made a conscious attempt to bring honor to the stockfish (dried salted cod). The most popular fish on the Iberian Peninsula, in this recipe the stockfish is first fried and then braised in a typical Catalan sauce, the *samfaina*. This dish is found on menus everywhere in and around Barcelona—especially in summer, when tomatoes and bell peppers are beautifully ripened by the sun.

*Samfaina* is the Iberian version of France's ratatouille. Onions and bell peppers are fried together until there is just a bit of bite left in the vegetables. Then garlic, tomatoes, and sautéed diced eggplants are added. There are other versions of *samfaina* that are made with zucchini or green bell peppers. It is also delicious served with chicken, pork, eggs, and snails.

By all means add a pinch of sugar to balance the acidity of the tomatoes. Coat the eggplants in flour before cooking, as this enables them to develop their full aroma and turn a delightful color while cooking.

After soaking the stockfish in cold water for 48 hours, the flesh will once again be soft and fairly salt-free. Stockfish (*bacalao* in Spanish) is salted and dried until as stiff as a board, and, in this form, it will keep for a long time. Today it is a classic in Iberian cuisine, although it does not come from local waters but has, since the 16th century, been caught by Spanish fishermen off the coasts of Canada and Newfoundland. It is not always worth a household buying a whole stockfish, so it is now also available filleted and vacuum-packed in portions for four people. The fish only needs to be soaked overnight.

*Place the stockfish in a bowl and cover in cold water. Soak for 48 hours, changing the water frequently. Pour off the water. Cut the meat into chunks, then coat in flour until completely covered.*

*Heat 7 tbsp (100 ml) of olive oil in a skillet and fry the fish, turning frequently, until golden all over. Set aside.*

*Halve the bell peppers, remove the pith and seeds, and chop the remainder into small pieces. Peel the onions and cut into evenly sized pieces. Heat 7 tbsp (100 ml) of olive oil in a pot. Sweat the bell peppers and onions for 15 minutes.*

# a la Samfaina

Add the whole peeled garlic cloves and the tomato quarters. Cover with a lid and cook until reduced to a samfaina.

Remove the stalks from the eggplants. Cut the flesh into strips. Dice the strips. Season with salt and coat in flour. Heat the remainder of the oil in a skillet until very hot, then fry the eggplants. Remove with a spatula, and add to the samfaina. Cover and cook for a further 10 minutes.

Arrange the pieces of stockfish in a pretty serving dish made of clay, and pour over the samfaina. Reheat on the top of the cooker. Serve very hot.

# Stockfish

| | |
|---|---|
| Preparation time: | 20 minutes |
| Soaking the stockfish: | 24–48 hours |
| Cooking time: | 1 hour 5 minutes |
| Difficulty: | ★★★ |

**Serves 4**

| | |
|---|---|
| 1³/₄ lb/800 g | stockfish |
| 14 oz/400 g | cauliflower |

| | |
|---|---|
| 2 cups/500 ml | olive oil |
| 4 cloves | garlic |
| 1 | onion |
| 2 cups/500 ml | fish stock (see pages 68 or 70 as an example) |
| 1 bunch | parsley |
| 4–5 | chive stalks |
| | salt |

Stockfish and cauliflower in a green sauce is a traditional Madrid dish. Those who are unable to afford hake are happy to use this as an inexpensive substitute.

Stockfish (dried salted cod) has played a special role in Spanish cuisine for centuries. Ever since America was discovered at the end of the 15th century, Basque fishermen have regularly set sail to fish for cod off the coast of Newfoundland to turn into stockfish. They made the dried fish popular all over the peninsula, especially as people living inland found it particularly useful during Lent because of its long shelf life.

Lots of Spaniards still buy their stockfish in special shops today. Depending on their preference, they opt for *bacalada* (the whole fish), *loncha* (the belly), *moro* and *lomo* (very fine square pieces), or simply *cola* (the tail), and occasionally just the *rosario* (rosary), the middle bones for soups.

The stockfish pieces used in this recipe should not be too thick. To soak them, fill a container with cold water and place the pieces in it. The gelatin between the fibers of the fish absorbs the liquid, which makes the meat swell. The cooked dish looks very attractive if, before cooking, you divide the cauliflower into rosettes the same size as the fish pieces.

Making the *salsa verde* (green sauce) calls for patience and skill. The pot needs to be turned slowly but continuously on the hob for 30 minutes, while the lukewarm oil is added. The gelatin leaves the fish fibers and blends with the oil to thicken the sauce.

*Cut the dried stockfish into pieces 1¹/₂–2 ins (3–4 cm) wide, and about 4 ins (10 cm) long. Soak in cold water for 24–48 hours.*

*Break the cauliflower into rosettes, and cut off the hard stalks. Blanch the rosettes in boiling salted water for 5 minutes, then scoop them out with a skimmer and set aside.*

*Heat a generous amount of olive oil in a pot. Sauté the thinly sliced garlic for 5 minutes, then remove and set aside. Pour off half the oil and reserve. Sweat the chopped onion in the remaining oil for 5 minutes.*

# with Cauliflower

Add the cauliflower and stockfish to the onions, and cook for about 30 minutes, turning the pot continuously and gradually adding the lukewarm oil. Add the reserved garlic oil at the end.

Pour the thickened sauce over the cauliflower and stockfish. Extend the sauce with fish stock, and simmer gently for 15 minutes, turning frequently.

Sprinkle with chopped parsley and chives. Arrange the fish and cauliflower on a plate. Whisk the sauce, then pour over the fish and vegetables. Garnish with the fried garlic.

# Tuna Fillet

Preparation time: 30 minutes
Cooking time: 40 minutes
Difficulty: ☆

**Serves 4**

| | |
|---|---|
| 1 | carrot |
| 1 | white turnip |
| 1 whole | garlic bulb |
| 1 | onion |
| 1 | green bell pepper |
| 1 | leek |

| | |
|---|---|
| 7 tbsp/100 ml | sherry vinegar |
| 7 tbsp/100 ml | white wine |
| 2 | bay leaves |
| 1 bunch | thyme |
| pinch | dried oregano |
| 1 tsp | ground cumin |
| 4 | cloves |
| 4 slices | red tuna, each weighing 6 oz/150 g |
| ¾ cup/200 ml | virgin olive oil |
| | salt and pepper |

For centuries, Spanish chefs have tried many different ways of preserving tuna without impairing its consistency or flavor. In a break from preserving fish in salt, they had the idea of preserving tuna in a marinade of vinegar, vegetables, and spices—*escabeche*. This cold sauce is used with every possible kind of fatty fish in Spain—including red tuna, sardines, and mackerel, as well as tuna. The abundance of fish oil in these varieties helps to preserve them, as well as enhance the flavor. Over time, this method of preservation has found its way, under various names, into the culinary traditions of other countries—including North Africa, Italy, South America, and even Belgium, which was once under Spanish rule.

Julio Reoyo recommends tuna in a delicious *escabeche*. At the time of the Moors, lookouts were positioned on towers to watch for the vast shoals of tuna. As soon as they were spotted in the vicinity of the coast, fishermen set sail and caught them in huge nets. For this recipe, Julio Reoyo likes to use fatty red tuna.

*Escabeche* always contains delicious vegetables. The vast, sun-drenched expanses of Castile provide the markets of Madrid with onions, garlic, bell peppers, tomatoes, eggplants, and much more. Garlic is a typical product of La Mancha. The Spanish consume nearly 3½ lb (1.5 kg) of it per person per year.

When you have put the sautéed tuna in the *escabeche*, transfer everything into a glass or plastic container. Sealed so it is airtight, the fish will keep for two or three months in the refrigerator. Serve cold or warm.

*Peel and slice the carrot. Peel and dice the turnip. Peel and roughly chop the garlic and onion. Cut the bell pepper and leek into chunks.*

*Put all the vegetables in a pot of water, and simmer gently for 15 minutes, stirring frequently. The vegetables should be well cooked.*

*Add the vinegar and white wine, and bring to the boil.*

# in Escabeche

Now put the spices in the pot: bay leaves, thyme, oregano, cumin, cloves, salt, and pepper. Add 2 cups (500 ml) cold water, and return to the boil.

Skin the tuna and cut into large chunks. Heat some oil in a skillet until very hot, then cook the tuna all over.

Put the tuna chunks into the boiling escabeche, and cook for 8 minutes. Then remove with a slotted spoon, and leave the liquid to cook. Serve the tuna in the warm escabeche.

# Fish Platter

Preparation time: *45 minutes*
Marinating time
  fish and squid: *1 hour*
Cooking time: *10–15 minutes*
Difficulty: ✶✶

**Serves 6**

| | |
|---|---|
| 12 | anchovies |
| 6 | sole fillets |
| 3 | red barbel |
| 3 | medium squid |
| 2 cups/500 ml | milk |

| | |
|---|---|
| 1³/₄ cups/200 g | flour |
| 2 cups/500 ml | peanut oil |
| 2 cloves | garlic |
| 3¹/₂ tbsp/50 ml | olive oil |
| 4–5 stalks | flat-leaf parsley |
| 5 | lemons |
| 2 | tomatoes (optional) |
| | salt and pepper |

**For the garnish (optional):**

| | |
|---|---|
| 3–4 | chive stalks |

Málaga is practically in the center of the Andalusian Mediterranean coast, and it has a major fishing harbor. The inhabitants love fried fish and seafood, and serve them in very many ways, either as hot entrées or delicious tapas.

Certain rules have to be observed when preparing the squid for this dish. Start by removing the head, which is connected to the abdominal organs. It is important that you also remove the transparent triangular support mechanism. Then wash the mantles thoroughly in running cold water, and rub them with your fingers to remove any residual sand or dirt. The mouth opening is situated in the middle of the tentacles. Press hard on the "beak" to push it out, and then cut it off. When filleting the red barbel, do not forget to remove the thin colored stripe. The very thin reddish skin, which is hard to remove, remains on the fish, and turns wonderfully crispy when fried.

Marinating in milk for an hour before cooking makes the fish fillets and squid wonderfully tender, and stops them from drying out when they are fried. However, it is important to pat them dry afterwards, otherwise hot fat will splash when they are frying. The flour coat should form only a thin layer around the fish. Shake off any excess flour when you turn it.

You can use groundnut oil or olive oil, or a combination of both, for deep frying. The advantage of groundnut oil is that it can be heated to a higher temperature, so the fish fillets turn beautifully yellow and crispy. Place the fried fish on paper towels to absorb the excess oil, and serve as hot as possible. Diced tomato adds color and a delicate sour touch to the garlic sauce.

*Cut the heads off the anchovies. Clean the fish, and remove the bones. Remove the sole fillets. Cut deeply into either side of the middle bone of the red barbel, and fillet from head to tail.*

*Remove the heads from the squid, and take out the insides. Empty the mantles completely using your fingers, and draw out the hard supporting mechanism. Skin, and wash everything thoroughly under running cold water.*

*Cut the squid crosswise into rings, and cut off the tentacles.*

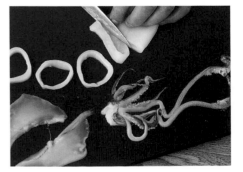

# from Málaga

Season the anchovies, squid rings, tentacles, sole, and red barbel with salt and pepper. Then place in a bowl of milk and marinate for an hour. Remove from the milk, and pat dry with paper towels. Coat in flour.

Heat the peanut oil in a pot until very hot. Deep fry the fish, squid, and tentacles for 6–7 minutes until golden.

Fry the thinly sliced garlic in olive oil for 5 minutes. Add the chopped parsley, salt, lemon juice, and skinned, chopped tomatoes. Arrange the fish fillets, sliced squid, and tentacles on plates. Serve garnished with chives and garlic sauce.

# Crayfish Rice

Preparation time: 20 minutes
Cooking time: 1 hour
Difficulty: ★★

**Serves 4**

| | |
|---|---|
| 1 | crayfish, approx. 2¾ lb/1.2 kg |
| 2 | dried red chile pods (pimiento ñora) |
| pinch | saffron threads |
| 1 lb 2 oz/500 g | rockfish (scorpion and gurnard, for example) and fish offcuts |

| | |
|---|---|
| 1 | fish stock bouillon cube |
| 2 whole | garlic bulbs |
| ⅔ cup/150 ml | olive oil |
| 4 tbsp | tomato paste |
| 3 cloves | fresh garlic, chopped |
| 10 oz/250 g | tiger shrimps, cleaned |
| 2 cups/400 g | rice |
| | salt |

**For the garnish:**

flat-leaf parsley

This clever recipe "in the style of Santa Pola" is typical of the town near Alicante, where there are numerous ways of preparing fish and seafood. This special dish combines lots of special aromas. Gourmets value crayfish for its firm yet tender white flesh. If you can, choose a medium-sized specimen.

For the dish to be a complete success, the stock must be prepared correctly. In the Alicante region, it is usually made from small, aromatic rockfish such as scorpion fish, gurnard, and various types of perch. Make sure you also take the offcuts (head, skin, tail, bones) when you buy your fish, as they will make the stock even tastier.

The Moors introduced rice-growing to Spain in the 8th century, and because of the proximity to the Ebro Delta the practice became widespread in the area around Alicante.

Cesar Marquiegui particularly recommends bomba, the variety grown in Calasparra, as the grains absorb plenty of liquid and yet retain their bite.

Saffron, the tiny stigma of a type of crocus, is essential for rice dishes such as this one, because it adds both aroma and color. The spice was introduced to Spain by its Arab occupiers. Today, more than 70 percent of the world's production is harvested in Castilia alone! October brings with it an incomparable sight, when entire fields of the mauve fall crocuses are in flower. The blue fields stretch as far as the eye can see, from Toledo to Albacete. Migrant workers gather to harvest the precious flowers. Often it is men who pick them, flower by flower. It is left to the women to remove the red stigma from the flowers, after which the stigma are roasted.

*Using a sharp knife, cut the crayfish in half from head to tail, then cut diagonally into pieces. Remove the seeds from the chile, and crush the saffron threads in a mortar.*

*To make the fish stock, set a large pot of water on to boil and add the rockfish, fish offcuts, and the bouillon cube. Bring to the boil, then cook for about 20 minutes.*

*Fry the whole garlic and the chile in 7 tbsp (100 ml) olive oil. Stir well, then add to the stock. Add the tomato paste and saffron, and cook for 15 minutes. Sieve, and season with salt.*

# Santa Pola

Heat the remainder of the olive oil in a paella pan. Fry the crayfish pieces, then remove and set aside.

Fry the 3 chopped garlic cloves and the prepared shrimps in the paella pan for about 2 minutes. Add the rice, and combine well.

Pour over 3¹/₄ cups (800 ml) fish stock, and simmer for about 18 minutes. Check the seasoning, then arrange the crayfish pieces on the rice. Bake in the oven (480 °F/250 °C) for 10 minutes, then leave to stand for 2 minutes. Garnish with parsley.

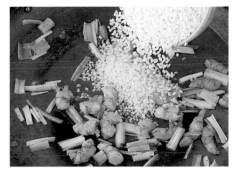

**Preparation time:** 40 minutes
**Cooking time:** 55 minutes
**Difficulty:** ★★

**Serves 4**

**For the paella:**

| | |
|---|---|
| 2 | leeks |
| 1 | carrot |
| 1 | head of celery |
| 1 bunch | scallions (spring onions) |
| 6 stalks | green asparagus |
| ³/₄ cup/150 g | tomatoes |
| 16 | river crayfish |
| 4 tbsp/60 ml | olive oil |
| 1 clove | garlic |
| 1 tsp | ground paprika |
| pinch | ground saffron |
| 1 cup/200 g | rice (ideally "Bomba") |
| | salt |

**For the river crayfish stock:**

| | |
|---|---|
| | green of 2 leeks |
| 1 | carrot |
| 2 | scallions (spring onions) |
| 1 | head of celery |
| 1 | tomato |
| 4 tbsp/60 ml | olive oil |
| 1 clove | garlic, halved |
| 3 sprigs | parsley |
| 1 | bay leaf |
| 4 | river crayfish |

**For the garnish:**

| | |
|---|---|
| | flat-leaf parsley |

This paella with river crayfish is an absolute delight; the original combination of delicate flavors make it the perfect highlight of a special meal shared with friends and family.

Every Spanish province along the Mediterranean has its own recipe for paella. Originally, the name *paella* referred only to the large skillet with two handles that was used for preparing rice. Rice, which is very popular in Spain, has been cultivated for about 6,000 years, and it was the Moors who brought it from India and China to the Iberian Peninsula.

The success of this recipe is determined by the quality of the rice and the olive oil. As a purist, Alberto Herráiz recommends round-grained bomba, which absorbs lots of liquid without losing its bite. This variety of rice comes from Calasparra, and it can absorb up to five times its own weight of liquid without bursting.

You really should make the stock for this recipe yourself using some river crayfish, because this will provide the aroma that makes the charm and flavor of the paella. Watch out for the measurements: always use twice as much liquid as rice.

River crayfish, which grow to between 5–6 inches (12–15 cm), are freshwater crustaceans. They used to be abundant in rivers and streams, but are quite rare today. Their delicate, aromatic meat is ideal for this dish. Depending on your preference and wallet, you can also use shrimp or lobster. Whatever you use, this Castilian feast will delight and impress your guests.

*Trim and roughly chop the vegetables for the stock. Cut the leeks, carrot, celery, and scallions into fine strips for the paella. Peel the asparagus. Purée the tomatoes.*

*Clean all the crayfish. Pull sharply on the middle tail fin, and remove the black thread from the inside.*

*To make the stock, fry the halved garlic clove in a large pot, and add the vegetables, parsley, and bay leaf. Add 4 of the crayfish, and simmer. Break the crayfish with a pestle. Cover with water, and simmer for 30 minutes. Strain.*

# River Crayfish

To make the paella: heat 4 tbsp (60 ml) of olive oil, and fry 1 whole garlic clove in it. Add the vegetable strips and halved asparagus stalks. Brown. Remove the garlic. Add the tomato purée. Stir well. Remove the skillet from the heat, and stir in the ground paprika.

Return to the heat, and pour over the strained stock. Stir in the saffron and plenty of salt. Stir in the rice. Cook over a high heat for 5 minutes. Lower the heat as soon as the rice rises to the surface.

Continue cooking the rice and vegetables in the oven (480 °F/250 °C) for 10 minutes. Place the river crayfish on the rice, and cook for a further 5 minutes. Serve the paella garnished with parsley leaves.

# Red Barbel

Preparation time: 35 minutes
Cooking time: 30 minutes
Difficulty: ✶

**Serves 4**

| | |
|---|---|
| 4 | small red barbel |
| ¾ cup/200 ml | olive oil |
| 1 | red bell pepper |
| 2 | potatoes |
| 2 | tomatoes |
| pinch | saffron thread |
| ½ | onion |

| | |
|---|---|
| 4 tbsp/60 ml | white wine |
| 2 tbsp/30 ml | pine nuts |
| 1 clove | garlic, chopped |
| 1 sprig | parsley |
| 2 | bay leaves |
| 4 | shrimp |
| | salt |

**For the fish stock:**

| | |
|---|---|
| 1 | tomato |
| 1 | leek |
| | offcuts from the red barbels (heads, tails, bones) |

This dish is typical of the town of Alicante. It is easy to prepare, and yet contains a mixture of aromas. It is usually served in a clay dish called *rustidera* in Spanish.

There is a lively fishing industry around Alicante. There are fishing villages everywhere, in which the culinary traditions are handed down from generation to generation. Red barbel is a rockfish, and its tasty firm flesh has many fans. The fish, which is easily identified by its pink to dark-red scaly skin, is available all year round from good fishmongers.

Red barbel has lots of small bones, but the meat is lean, fine, and extremely delicious. The smaller the fish, the more aromatic they are. If red barbel is not available, you can use turbot, another popular, high-quality fish, instead.

The village of Dénia is near Alicante. It is famous for its excellent, dark-red "gambas." These wonderful shrimp are usually served simply *a la plancha*, on a red-hot skillet brushed with olive oil, and eaten as tapas. In this recipe, though, they are baked in the oven with the other ingredients. If you are unable to obtain shrimp, you can substitute clams.

The sophisticated and independent culinary tradition of the region of Alicante is also evident in the addition of pine nuts, a popular ingredient in many local dishes. These long kernels are the fruit of various pine trees that grow around the Mediterranean. Their resinous, nutty flavor is similar to that of almonds, but the mild aroma and softer consistency make them ideal for use in all kinds of fish dishes.

*Clean the red barbel and scrape off the scales. Cut off the heads and tails, and set aside for the stock. Cut crosses into the flesh on one side of the fish. Season with salt, brush with olive oil, then broil quickly under the broiler.*

*Roughly chop the tomato and leek for the stock. Cook the leek, tomatoes, and red barbel offcuts in a large pot of water for about 20 minutes. Then strain the stock.*

*Remove the seeds from the bell peppers, and cut into strips. Peel and thinly slice the potatoes. Slice the tomato. Crush the saffron in a mortar.*

# from Alicante

Peel and thinly slice the halved onion, and fry in a pot with 7 tbsp (100 ml) olive oil. Fry the bell pepper strips, sliced potatoes, and tomatoes separately in the remainder of the oil.

Add the potatoes, bell pepper, and tomatoes to the onions, and pour over the white wine. Add the saffron threads, and season with salt.

Add the pine nuts, chopped garlic, parsley, and bay leaf. Arrange the cleaned shrimp and the pre-cooked red barbel on the vegetables. Pour over the stock. Bake in the over (350 °F/180 °C) for 8 minutes. Arrange on plates.

# Catalan

| Preparation time: | 35 minutes |
|---|---|
| Cooking time: | 1 hour |
| Difficulty: | ★★ |

**Serves 4**

| | |
|---|---|
| 2 | lobsters |
| ⅞ cup/100 g | flour |
| 2 | large onions |
| 4 | ripe tomatoes |

| | |
|---|---|
| 2 cloves | garlic |
| ¾ cup/200 ml | olive oil |
| 4 | potatoes |
| 2 cups/500 ml | fish stock (see pages 68 or 70 as an example) |
| 3½ tbsp/50 g | almonds, skinned and roasted |
| 1 bunch | parsley, chopped |
| pinch | saffron threads |
| | salt and pepper |

This lobster dish is one of the figureheads of Catalan cuisine. If you are unable to obtain lobster—*llamàntol* in Catalan—you can use other fish or crustaceans instead, such as angler fish, hake, crayfish, scampi, and rockfish.

For this recipe, Pep Masiques combines two characteristic elements in Catalan cuisine—namely *picada*, and *sofrito* (also known as *sofregit*). The latter is the alpha and omega of this method of preparation: a thick sauce made of onions and tomatoes, fried in oil and seasoned with garlic (reserve some for the *picada* when you are frying it). You can use the tomatoes with or without the skins, whichever you prefer. Add a pinch of sugar to balance the acidity if required.

Spicy *picada* is one of Catalonia's most popular sauces, and is served with many fish and meat dishes. It is made of toasted almonds, which can be replaced by filberts, pine nuts, or even raisins, and parsley, garlic, saffron, and olive oil. Our chef combines everything in a mortar, cleverly wrapping it in a clean towel to prevent any of the contents from escaping.

Pep Masiques also had the brilliant idea of enhancing the *picada* with the liquid that is obtained when cutting up the lobster. It sets quickly when surrounded by air, so it will also thicken the sauce. What's more, it adds an incomparable aroma. You can substitute a fish stock bouillon cube, a little wine, or even some breadcrumbs if you prefer. Pep Masiques spoons the *picada* over the potatoes, and places the lobster pieces on top of them. Garnish the dish with a little parsley, and serve in the dish it is cooked in.

Place the lobster on a board and cut through lengthwise, inserting the knife behind the head and cutting through as far as the tail. Save the liquid that emerges for the picada. Remove the head.

Sprinkle the flour on a plate. Coat the lobster halves all over until they are completely covered. Peel and finely chop the onions for the sofrito. Skin and quarter the tomatoes. Peel and finely chop the garlic.

Fry the garlic in olive oil in a roasting pan for 5 minutes, then remove and set aside for the picada. Now fry the lobster pieces for 20 minutes, then remove and set aside. Fry the chopped onions and tomato in the same dish for 10 minutes.

# Lobster

Peel and thinly slice the potatoes. Put in the roasting pan with the onions and tomatoes, and season with salt and pepper. Pour over the fish stock. Cook over a high heat for 10 minutes until the potatoes are ready.

To make the picada, crush the almonds, chopped parsley, and fried garlic in a mortar with some salt and the saffron. Blend well, then add to the reserved lobster juices.

Add 2 tbsp of picada to the cooked potatoes. Place the lobster halves on top, and heat over a high heat for 5 minutes. Serve very hot in the roasting pan.

# Titaina Salad

Preparation time: 30 minutes
Cooking time: 30 minutes
Difficulty: ★

**Serves 4**

| | |
|---|---|
| 1³/₄ lb/800 g | fillets from fatty red tuna |
| 2 cloves | garlic |
| 1 cup/200 g | plum tomatoes |
| 1 bunch | parsley |
| 1 cup/200 g | red bell peppers |
| 2 | eggplants |

| | |
|---|---|
| 1 cup/250 ml | olive oil |
| pinch | sugar |
| 2¹/₂ tbsp/40 g | pine nuts |
| | salt and pepper |

**For the vinaigrette:**

| | |
|---|---|
| 1 | diced tomato |
| 1 bunch | basil, fried in oil |
| | a few pine nuts |
| | olive oil |
| | balsamic vinegar |

Of all the traditional dishes served in Valencia, *titaina* is the most popular. Canned tuna is sometimes added to this salad of bell peppers, eggplants, tomatoes, and pine nuts. Oscar Torrijos likes to serve it with a nice tuna fish fillet *a la plancha*—that is to say, broiled on a red-hot skillet that has been brushed with olive oil, transforming it into an unbeatable culinary experience.

The chef's preferred choice is red tuna, a huge fish that can weigh up to 550 lb (250 kg) and is found in most of the world's oceans—including the Mediterranean, the Atlantic, the Pacific, and the Indian Ocean. In gastronomy, the belly is considered the best part because it is large and full of healthy fish oil.

To skin the fillet, Oscar Torrijos puts it on a chopping board, and runs a very sharp knife between the skin and the flesh. He then carefully cuts diagonally through the fillet to half the thickness so the top is marked with a grid, which makes the tuna look particularly appetizing. Do not cook the fish for too long, as it will become dry. It should be served rare.

The chef places the fish fillet on a piece of baking parchment to wrap it around the *titaina*. Alternatively, you could also use a sushi mat as is used in Japanese cooking. Although this is not necessarily the Spanish option, it does work.

To add the final touch to the dish, fry a few basil leaves in oil and use them to garnish the fish before serving.

*Place the tuna fish on a chopping board. Remove the skin, using a large knife. Slice the fish diagonally, cutting against the grain. Halve each piece horizontally, reserving any leftovers.*

*Peel and chop the garlic. Skin the tomatoes, then cut them into quarters, remove the seeds, and dice the flesh. Chop the parsley. Cut the bell peppers, and remove the pith and seeds. Chop the remainder into small pieces. Do the same with the eggplants.*

*Sauté the diced bell pepper in oil for 5 minutes. Sauté the tomatoes and the salt, pepper, and sugar in oil in a pot for 5 minutes. Fry the garlic in oil in a second skillet. Add the eggplants, and cook for 5 minutes. Season with salt and pepper. Then drain on paper towels.*

# with Tuna

Using your fingers, brush the sliced tuna fish with oil, then fry in very hot oil for 3 minutes. Turn with a metal spatula, and fry for 3 minutes on the other side. Season with salt.

Fry the pine nuts in oil for 3–4 minutes. Add the chopped parsley, and combine well. Add the chopped eggplants, bell pepper, and tuna pieces. Simmer well for 5 minutes, stirring frequently, and you have your titaina salad.

Place a tuna fish fillet on a piece of baking parchment. Spread a little of the salad on top and roll up into a sausage shape. Arrange a circle of salad on the plates, and place a tuna fish roll on top. Serve with the vinaigrette made from the ingredients listed on page 120.

# Tiznao

Preparation time: 25 minutes
Soaking time for
  the stockfish: 24 hours
Cooking time: 2 hours
Difficulty: ✩

**Serves 4**

2¼ lb/1 kg  stockfish
1 lb 14 oz/800 g  onions
1 lb 14 oz/800 g  red bell peppers
1 clove  garlic

**For the spicy sauce:**
6½ tbsp/100 ml  olive oil
2 tbsp/30 ml  sherry vinegar
1 tsp  dried oregano
½ tbsp  ground paprika
  (pimientón)
  black pepper

**For the garnish:**
  fresh oregano
  ground paprika
  (pimientón)

To the Castilians of La Mancha, *tiznao* (literally translated as "glowing embers") is always associated with stockfish. The traditional recipe is usually cooked on a Friday (the day on which devout Catholics refrain from eating meat), and of course during Lent. The period of abstinence between Ash Wednesday and Easter Sunday has always been taken seriously in Spain.

The deeply religious Spanish have therefore made stock-fish—*bacalao*—a Lent dish par excellence. Salted, dried coldwater cod has been at home on the Iberian Peninsula since the 17th century, and is used in many delicious dishes.

It is important to soak the stockfish for 24 hours. Alberto Herráiz advises covering the dish with plastic wrap and putting it in the refrigerator, and changing the water several times during the soaking period.

*Tiznao* is an ancient recipe. The ingredients used to be cooked over an open fire. The glowing embers helped to remove the salt from the stockfish, and smoked the other ingredients at the same time.

This very healthy dish with lots of Mediterranean flair is based primarily on red bell peppers. These garden fruits, which are pampered by the sun, are delicious raw or cooked, with or without their skins. The skin is easy to remove if you broil the bell peppers first. Red bell peppers contain a great deal of vitamins A and C, and the flesh is crunchy, and mildly aromatic. Make sure the peppers you choose are firm and smooth with a hard, green stalk.

The aroma of the *tiznao* is produced by the onions, liliaceous plants that have been cultivated for over 5,000 years, and came originally from northern Asia. The large, yellow onion—or Spanish onion—is particularly mild.

*The evening before, cut the stockfish into pieces. Soak in cold water. Wrap the peeled onions, bell peppers, garlic, and stockfish individually in aluminum foil, and bake in the oven (300 °F/150 °C): stockfish and bell peppers for 15 minutes, garlic and onions for 2 hours.*

*Remove the bones from the stockfish and separate the flesh into pieces. Reserve some of the flakes for the garnish.*

*Combine the olive oil, sherry vinegar, dried oregano, ground paprika, and black pepper, and whisk with a balloon whisk.*

Using a sharp knife, skin the bell peppers and remove the seeds. Cut the flesh into thin slices.

Thinly slice the onions. Cut the roast garlic cloves in half lengthwise, and, using the knife blade, squeeze out the soft flesh.

Combine the stockfish, bell peppers, onions, and garlic in a bowl. Pour over the sauce, and combine well. Arrange on plates. Put a few flakes of stockfish on each plate. Garnish with oregano, and dust with ground paprika.

# Trout with

Preparation time: 40 minutes
Cooking time: 20 minutes
Difficulty: ★

**Serves 4**

| | |
|---|---|
| 2¼ lb/1 kg | salmon trout |
| 1 | red bell pepper |
| 2 | small artichokes |
| 3 | scallions (spring onions) |
| 8 slices | Serrano ham |

| | |
|---|---|
| 2 cloves | garlic |
| 1 cup/250 ml | olive oil |
| | salt and pepper |

**For the sauce:**

| | |
|---|---|
| 6½ tbsp/100 ml | sherry vinegar |
| 3½ tbsp/50 g | honey |
| ½ | vanilla bean |
| ½ | cinnamon stick |

The Castilians have a real passion for trout and ham. Many of the aficionados of this traditional dish spend hours discussing whether and how to combine Serrano ham with trout: should the fish be wrapped in the ham, or just garnished with it? Alberto Herráiz serves the trout wrapped in a coat of ham.

Alberto Herráiz remains true to the culinary traditions of his first home even while living in his second home, Paris. In his restaurant "Fogón"—"hearth fire"—he has perfected the art of preparing rice. However, the trout packages are a silent passion of his. Always creative and bursting with ideas, our chef complements this familiar dish with a sweet sauce and fine vegetables. This harmonious variant is a complete success, and a delightful homage to Castile.

In Central Spain, trout are still caught with a fly. Fishermen and gourmets alike appreciate river trout for its fine, fatty, and absolutely delicious meat. Spicy Serrano ham goes wonderfully with it. The typically Spanish mountain ham from free-roaming pigs is still made using traditional methods. The ham is left to dry in the open air for at least a year, during which it develops its incomparable aroma.

Easy as the dish is to prepare, it has plenty of character. The sweet sauce, scented with cinnamon, vanilla, honey, and sherry vinegar, creates a delightful balance to the other ingredients.

Alberto Herráiz chooses artichokes, bell peppers, and fresh scallions—which add a spring-like flair—to go with this dish.

*To make the sauce, heat the sherry vinegar, honey, vanilla, and cinnamon in a pot. Reduce by half, and then set aside.*

*Remove the fins from the trout, then fillet the fish and skin it. Use a pair of tweezers to remove all the bones. Broil the bell pepper for 10 minutes, and skin it. Cut off all the leaves of the artichoke. Peel the scallions, reserving the green as garnish.*

*Spread a slice of ham on a chopping board, place a piece of trout fillet on top, and wrap it up in the ham. Peel the garlic.*

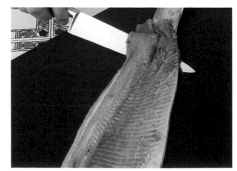

# Serrano Ham

Heat the oil in a skillet, and fry the trout packages for about 2 minutes. Remove and set aside.

Pour away half of the oil. Still using the same skillet, fry the artichoke hearts, the scallion segments, and the garlic. Combine well, then add the bell peppers. Continue cooking, stirring continuously.

Season lightly with salt and pepper. Use the sauce to dissolve the cooking juices. Place the trout packages on a plate, and surround with the sauce. Arrange the vegetables on the side. Garnish with the finely chopped green of the onions.

# Meat & Poultry

# Rack of Lamb with

Preparation time: 1 hour
Cooking time: 1 hour 30 minutes
Difficulty: ★

**Serves 4**

| | |
|---|---|
| 2 | racks of lamb, each with 12 cutlets |
| 1 | carrot |
| 1 | onion |
| 1 | tomato |
| 1 | leek |
| ²/₃ cup/150 ml | olive oil |

| | |
|---|---|
| ³/₄ cup/200 ml | red wine |
| 1 sprig | rosemary |
| 3¹/₂ tbsp/100 g | honey |
| 4 tbsp/60 ml | red wine vinegar |
| | salt and pepper |

**For the garnish:**

| | |
|---|---|
| 8 | mini carrots |
| 8 | mini turnips |
| 8 | mini zucchini |
| 4 oz/100 g | sugar peas |

Way back in the 15th century, the Muslim population of Córdoba used to cook roast lamb with honey and aromatic herbs on special occasions. Following the Reconquista in 1492, the region found itself under Spanish-Christian rule once again, but this recipe has survived until today.

Alberto Herráiz is proud of his home, and he chooses high-quality, award-winning lamb of controlled origin for this dish. The animals roam free in La Mancha in the heart of Spain. The method described here does credit to the quality of the meat. The chef believes that the rack is the best cut for this recipe, but the loin is an excellent substitute.

To make the most of the sauce, our chef adds red wine from La Mancha to the cooking juices and vegetables. It is a fairly heavy wine, and so is ideal for reducing the sauce.

Alberto Herráiz uses a wine vinegar based on a Cabernet-Sauvignon, which can also be replaced by a mild red wine vinegar. The vinegar for this sauce should not be too acidic. One further enhancement to the delicate rosemary aroma of the rack of lamb is rosemary honey. If you find the sauce has not reduced sufficiently after braising the vegetables and bones, the chef advises straining the liquid through a sieve and boiling it again until reduced. You can also dust the bones in flour before putting the roasting pan in the oven.

A good winter side dish to go with the rack of lamb is steamed potatoes, whereas spring vegetables are ideal in that season.

*Peel the little carrots and turnips, and pare the zucchini in strips. Blanch the sugar peas until just firm to the bite, then plunge them in cold water. Blanch the zucchini on their own, then blanch the carrots and turnips together.*

*Trim the meat from between the top of the bones of the racks of lamb. Using a small knife, cut into the meat along the spine, then use a cleaver to separate it from the rack. Set aside the racks. Cut off the fat.*

*Trim and peel the carrot, onion, tomato, and leek. Chop the lamb's backbone into pieces. Put the vegetables and bones in a casserole with a little oil, and brown for 15 minutes.*

# Honey and Rosemary

As soon as the vegetables start to change color, pour over the red wine, then add the rosemary, salt, and pepper. Put the casserole in the oven (480 °F/250 °C) for about 1 hour, until the vegetables and meat are very soft.

Season the racks with salt and pepper, and brown on all sides in a skillet. Put the skillet in the oven. Cook for a further 6 minutes, turning occasionally.

Remove the casserole from the oven. Stir in the honey and vinegar, strain, then reduce to thicken the sauce. Slice the racks of lamb. Serve the cutlets with the blanched mini-vegetables, honey and wine sauce.

# Young Goat Cutlets

Preparation time: 25 minutes
Cooking time: 15 minutes
Difficulty: ✶

**Serves 4**

| | |
|---|---|
| 2¼ lb /1 kg | rack of baby goat |
| 1 bunch | fresh garlic |
| 1⅔ cups/400 ml | olive oil |
| 3 | large potatoes |
| | salt |

The village of Villena near Alicante is famous for its garlic production. The Spaniards love the bulb for its piquancy, and so it is hardly surprising that it should appear in so many dishes.

This dish was invented by goatherders. The main ingredient is young goat. Goats are bred mainly in the Verga Baja region near Murcia. The meat from these young animals is usually available from mid-March to early May. Young goat tastes a little like milk-fed lamb, which makes a perfect substitute.

The olive oil, in particular, gives the baby goat cutlets in this recipe the most wonderful aroma. Olive oil is used everywhere in Spanish gastronomy. The Iberians are great lovers of the fine oil, and know everything there is to know about the various qualities and flavors.

In this sun-drenched country, the oil is usually a little tart, but always very mild and fruity. Anyone who values a high-quality product needs to look out for three things: that it is produced in olive groves, that it is harvested by hand, and that it is pressed appropriately. The most renowned is *aciete de oliva virgen extra*—that is to say, the extra virgin oil from the first cold pressing.

Olive oil must be kept cool and out of the light, ideally in a glass bottle or clay jug. Direct sunlight will shorten its shelf life, and reduce the levels of vitamins and nutrients.

Potatoes are grown along the entire Mediterranean coast, from Gerona to Málaga. This root vegetable, which came originally from South America, is one of the staples in the modern diet. Choose ones that are firm and smooth with no obvious shoots.

*Trim the meat, cutting the meat off the ribs along the entire length, and cutting out the meat between the ribs. Scrape all the meat off the bones.*

*Chop off the outer end of the ribs with a cleaver. Divide the rack into cutlets with a sharp knife.*

*Peel the garlic, then cut it into pieces. Season with salt, and fry in olive oil. Set the garlic aside, and use the oil for the cutlets.*

# from Villena

Peel the potatoes. Slice very thinly using a mandoline, then cut these slices into matchsticks.

Fry the potato strips in the remainder of the olive oil, and drain on paper towels to absorb the excess oil. Season with salt.

Season the young goat cutlets with salt, and fry in the garlic-flavored olive oil. Arrange 2 cutlets with a little garlic and some of the potatoes on plates.

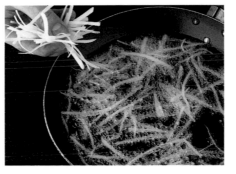

# Sirloin with

Preparation time: 15 minutes
Cooking time: 10 minutes
Difficulty: ☆

**Serves 4**

**For the steak:**
2¼ lb/800 g    beef sirloin
3 tbsp/45 ml    olive oil

**For the sauce:**
1⅔ cups/400 g    crème fraîche
8 oz/200 g    Tresviso cheese
2 tsp    cornstarch
   salt and black pepper

(Crème fraîche can be made at home by combining 1 cup whipping cream and 2 tbsp buttermilk in a glass container. Stir well, cover and let stand at room temperature (70 °F/21°C) from 8 to 24 hours, or until very thick.)

**For the accompaniments:**
2–3    mild green chiles
4    potatoes
4 tbsp/60 ml    olive oil
   salt and pepper

Cheeses from Spain and Latin America usually have a second name that describes their texture, aroma, or origin, such as *quesa de bola* (ball-shaped cow's milk cheese), *quesa de cabra* (goat's cheese), or the typical Asturian specialty, *queso de cabrales*, a blue cheese made of cow's and sheep's milk. The *queso de Tresviso* used here is an extremely original companion to beef steak. It is a spicy, tasty Spanish blue cheese, not to be confused with Italy's *treviso*. The Basques eat it as it is, but it is ideal for tasty sauces such as this one.

The sauce made of the cheese and crème fraîche is wonderfully creamy. Rufino Manjarrès advises you to check it before adding the second piece of cheese. The strong smell of the cheese melting in the cream is a pleasant sensation. Our chef has a preference for fine, smooth sauces with lots of flavor, which is why he strains the sauce through a pointed sieve to make the consistency perfect. This means there is no chance at all of unsightly lumps ruining the end effect!

The tender beef sirloin goes surprisingly well with the hearty sauce, but do make this dish with red meat only. The chef advises against serving it with a light meat, as its flavor would be lost, the fine balance between the aromas of the meat and cheese destroyed.

The potatoes are diced, then fried in olive oil. They go extremely well with this dish. Tiny pieces of chile added at the last minute give it an additional "kick."

*Cut the sirloin into 1 in (2 cm) thick slices, and set aside.*

*Bring half the crème fraîche to the boil. As soon as it begins to bubble, add all of the cheese at once, and stir well. Add the remainder of the crème fraîche, and bubble gently for 5 minutes at low heat until the cheese has completely melted.*

*Dissolve the starch in a glass of cold water. Remove the cheese sauce from the heat, then blend in the dissolved cornstarch. Season with salt and pepper, and stir well. Simmer gently for 1 more minute to allow it to thicken.*

# Cheese Sauce

Strain the sauce through a pointed sieve. Repeat, if necessary, until the sauce is completely smooth and silky. Keep warm.

Quickly fry the pieces of sirloin in very hot olive oil for 3 minutes if you want them rare on the inside.

Arrange 5–6 slices of meat on each plate, pour over the cheese sauce, and serve with the chile fried potatoes.

# Meatballs

Preparation time: 45 minutes
Cooking time: 1 hour
Difficulty: ★

**Serves 4**

| | |
|---|---|
| 1¼ cups/300 ml | olive oil |
| ⅛ cup/15 g | flour |
| ½ | green bell pepper |
| ½ | red bell pepper |
| 1 each | carrot, tomato, onion |
| 1 clove | garlic |
| 1 sprig | thyme |
| 1 | bay leaf |
| 8 oz/200 g | squid |
| 4 tbsp/60 ml | white wine |

| | |
|---|---|
| 1 tsp/5 ml | Spanish brandy |
| | salt |

**For the meatball mixture:**

| | |
|---|---|
| 1¼ lb/600 g | ground veal |
| 7 oz/200 g | ground pork |
| 1 | unwaxed lemon |
| 1 bunch | chives |
| 10 | pine nuts |
| 1 clove | garlic, chopped |
| 1 slice | light country bread |
| 1 | egg |
| | freshly ground nutmeg |
| | salt and black pepper |

This braised dish of meatballs and squid, called *estofado* in Spanish, is a specialty of Catalonia. It cleverly combines the aromas of land and sea, and is well known and loved beyond the borders of Catalonia. In Alicante on the Mediterranean coast, this hearty dish is particularly popular in winter.

Squid, or *sepia*, is identified by its sack-like, gray-beige body, its sides ending in a thin fin seam. Inside is a hard calcium shell, the cuttlebone, which has to be removed before the squid is cooked. Ten tentacles grow from the relatively large head, two of which are considerably longer than the other eight. Depending on what is available at the time, you can also use smaller ones.

Tomatoes and bell peppers are grown in the area around Alicante, and add strong aromas to a dish. These are complemented by the onion, which came originally from Northern Asia. Buy milder Spanish onions. A tip to spare your eyes: put the onions in the refrigerator for an hour, then pour boiling water over them to make them easier to peel.

Cesar Marquiegui combines squid with meatballs made of ground veal and pork. The ground meat is flavored with lemon peel, garlic, egg, and bread, and seasoned with ground nutmeg. This spice, which game from the East Indies, is always used freshly ground, and should be stored in an airtight container.

Another ingredient is chives, which adds a gentle peppery note to the dish. Chives contain lots of vitamins, and are available fresh from spring to fall. The stalks should be bright green and firm, and not yet flowering.

*Combine the ground meats. Season with grated lemon peel and salt. Add the chopped chives, pine nuts, and chopped garlic. Remove the crust from the bread, then soak the bread. Add it and the egg to the meat. Season with nutmeg and pepper. Knead until smooth.*

*Oil your hands lightly, then shape small balls from the meat mixture. Coat them in flour.*

*Heat ¾ cup (200 ml) oil in a skillet, and fry the meatballs until brown. Remove, place on paper towels to absorb excess oil, and set aside.*

# with Sepia

Finely chop the bell peppers, carrot, tomato, onion, and garlic. Fry in a pot in the remainder of the oil. Add the thyme, bay leaf, and salt.

Clean the squid, and remove the cuttlebone. Cut the body and tentacles into pieces, and add to the vegetables. Season with salt, and stir.

Add the white wine and brandy. Cook for 2 minutes. Sprinkle over 1 tbsp of flour, and stir. Pour over water to cover, and bring to the boil. Simmer for 40 minutes. Add the meatballs, and continue cooking for 10 minutes. Arrange on plates and serve.

# Loin of Pork

Preparation time: 20 minutes
Cooking time: 20 minutes
Difficulty: ★

**Serves 4**

| | |
|---|---|
| 2¼ lb/1 kg | pork fillet, ideally from Iberian pigs |
| 20 | fresh pearl onions |
| 7 tbsp/100 ml | olive oil |

| | |
|---|---|
| 2 cups/500 ml | dry sherry |
| 2 cups/500 ml | meat stock |
| pinch | flour (optional) |
| | fresh thyme |
| | salt and pepper |

Tenderloin of pork in a tasty sherry sauce is a treat for the palate—and it doesn't require much in the way of preparation. The ingredients are available all year round. Iberian pigs are known for the excellent quality of their marbled flesh, which has nothing in common with that of their farmed cousins. This is because they are allowed to roam free. They are bred mainly in the south-west of Spain, from Salamanca to Cádiz. The skin and bristles of these sturdy animals are usually dark, the body slim and elongated. They have adapted particularly well to the dry climate of southern Spain. They live mainly in the region of Dehesa, in light forests of cork and stone oak with meadows between. In winter they feed on acorns and other fruits of the forest, in the spring on meadow grasses. Their meat is popular as ham, chorizo, and so on.

For this recipe, the chef chose loin of pork (*filet mignon*), which is considered the finest part of the pig. It comes from the tenderloin on the back. You can dust the meat with a little flour before cooking. This will help the surface to brown, and make it nice and crisp. It also binds the sauce a little. The meat should still be slightly pink on the inside when cooked. You can cut it into thinner medallions if you prefer.

Sherry enhances the sauce with its fine, fresh aroma. This Andalusian wine is produced in Jerez de le Frontera, Sanlúcar de Barrameda, and El Puerto de Santa María. Although it is called Jerez in Spain, it is sometimes referred to on the Iberian Peninsula by its English name, "sherry." You could, if you prefer, use a white wine of your choice.

*Use a sharp knife to trim off any skin and excess fat from the meat. Cut the meat in half, then season with salt and pepper.*

*Peel the onions. Fry the meat in a skillet in very hot olive oil, then add the onions.*

*As soon as the meat and onions are cooked, pour off most of the cooking juices.*

# in Sherry

Pour the sherry into the remainder of the juices, and reduce over a high heat.

Pour over the stock, then put in the oven for 5 minutes.

Cut the meat into slices, and serve very hot. Garnish with thyme leaves.

# Fricassee with

Preparation time: 30 minutes
Cooking time: 1 hour 15 minutes
Difficulty: ★★

**Serves 4**

| | |
|---|---|
| 1 | oven-ready chicken |
| 1¼ cups/150 g | flour |
| ¾ cup/200 ml | olive oil |
| 1 | onion, finely chopped |

| | |
|---|---|
| ¾ cup/200 ml | dry white wine |
| ½ cup/50 g | walnuts |
| 1 bunch | parsley, chopped |
| ¾ cup/200 ml | milk |
| 4 cups/1 l | chicken stock |
| 1 whole | garlic bulb |
| 2 | eggs |
| ½ | baguette |
| | salt and pepper |

Chicken fricassee, with its appetizing sauce of walnuts and parsley, chopped eggs, and croutons, is a popular dish on the menus of luxury restaurants. The walnuts in this dish make it typical of Madrid; other parts of the Iberian Peninsula use chopped almonds instead.

Julio Reoyo finds that light meats work best in this dish. However, you could also use a large, fattier poularde—or even a spring chicken. With this dish, it is not so much the weight classification that matters, especially as Spanish chickens don't usually end up in the pot until the end of their egg-laying careers. Just make sure the bird has plenty of tender meat.

Singe off any feathers left on the skin with a gas torch. The chef separates the wings and quarters, then divides the latter into thighs and drumsticks. The carcass is cut in half. Finally, everything is coated in flour so it turns nice and crisp when frying. The flour will also thicken the sauce a little.

As is customary in Spain, the slices of bread are deep-fried in plenty of oil. As soon as they are golden on one side, turn them over and fry the other side. Remove from the oil and place on paper towels to absorb the excess.

This traditional dish from Madrid is one of the so-called *guisos*, as ragouts are called in Spanish. Like all braised dishes, it tastes even better reheated the next day.

*Place the chicken on a chopping board, and cut into 8 pieces with a large knife. Season with salt and freshly ground black pepper.*

*Sprinkle the flour on a plate, then coat the chicken pieces completely.*

*Fry the chicken in a casserole in 6½ tbsp (100 ml) oil over very high heat, turning each piece so they all brown evenly. Set aside. Sauté the finely chopped onion in the same oil for 5 minutes. Return the chicken to the casserole, and pour over the white wine.*

# Walnut Sauce

Crush the walnuts and chopped parsley in a mortar, then pour in the milk. Pour this mixture over the chicken.

Add the chicken stock. Bring to the boil, and cook for about 45 minutes.

Boil the eggs for 10 minutes, then run cold water over them, and peel. Slice the bread, and fry in the remaining olive oil for 5 minutes. Serve the fricassee very hot. Garnish with the bread and chopped hard-boiled eggs.

# Leg of Lamb

| | |
|---|---|
| *Preparation time:* | *30 minutes* |
| *Soaking time:* | *30 minutes* |
| *Marinate:* | *overnight* |
| *Cooking time:* | *1 hour 15 minutes* |
| *Difficulty:* | ★★ |

**Serves 6**

| | |
|---|---|
| 3 tbsp | raisins |
| 3 tbsp/45 ml | sherry |

| | |
|---|---|
| 3 lb 6 oz/1.5 kg | loin of milk-fed lamb |
| 12 | dates |
| 2 tbsp | whole peeled almonds |
| ½ tsp | ground cinnamon |
| ½ tsp | ground cumin |
| 2 cups/500 ml | olive oil |
| 2 | large onions, chopped |
| 2 cloves | garlic |
| 2 cups/500 ml | chicken stock |
| | salt and pepper |

This finely flavored loin of lamb with raisins, as prepared by Javier Valero, is reminiscent of the lavish cuisine of Morocco. "Lamb Moorish-style"—or *Cordero a la moruña*, to give it its Spanish name—takes us back to the time when the Moors ruled over Andalusia—an extraordinary period of cultural blossoming, when exquisite culinary delights found their way to the Iberian Peninsula.

This festive dish is particularly tasty if you use meat from milk-fed lambs. In Spain, lambs are slaughtered at an early age, before they have been weaned. This makes the meat very light, and the whole animal weighs no more than 11–13 lb (5–6 kg). The "crib" of milk-fed lambs and piglets is the region to the north-west of Madrid, around Segovia, and in Madrid in particular people often visit restaurants just to enjoy these specialties provided by masters of their craft.

It is important to leave the leg in the marinade for a while, to enable it to absorb the flavor of the spices and the olive oil.

The dried fruit adds a delicate, sweet touch to the dish, especially the sherry-soaked raisins, which come from near Málaga. They are then braised with the meat, during which time they become wonderfully juicy. You can also use dried apricots, prunes, or even apples instead of the raisins, and the sherry can be replaced by Málaga, an old, sweet wine from Andalusia.

In Andalusia, as in Maghreb cuisine, raisins, almonds, and dates are often used in hearty dishes. In the Middle Ages, the Moors in the south of Spain were also the first to grow almonds in Spain, in addition to citrus fruit, apricots, quince, and pistachios.

*The evening before, soak the raisins in sherry for about 30 minutes. Bone the leg of lamb, and cut the meat into fairly large pieces.*

*Place the pieces of meat in a bowl, and add the soaked raisins, dates, almonds, cinnamon, and cumin.*

*Add 1¼ cups (300 ml) olive oil, salt, pepper, chopped onions, and garlic, and rub well into the meat. Marinate overnight.*

# Moorish-style

The next day, heat the remainder of the olive oil until really hot. Fry the meat pieces in a casserole for 5–10 minutes.

Add the fruits and the remaining ingredients for the marinade, and fry over a high heat, stirring continuously.

Pour over the chicken stock and bring to the boil. Cover, and cook for 1 hour until the meat is cooked and tender. Remove the meat from the casserole, and cut into slices. Arrange with the dried fruit and the sauce. Garnish with raisins.

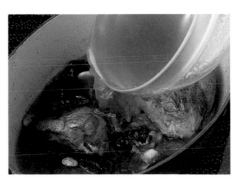

# Veal Cheeks

| Preparation time: | 45 minutes |
|---|---|
| Cooking time: | 4 hours |
| Difficulty: | ★ |

**Serves 4**

| 4 | veal cheeks |
|---|---|
| ³/₄ cup/200 ml | olive oil |
| 1 tsp | veal stock concentrate |
| 2 | red onions |
| 2 | tomatoes |
| 2 | leeks |
| 1 bulb | garlic |

| 4 | mild chile peppers (*pimientos choriceros*) |
|---|---|
| 1 75 cl bottle | Rioja |
| 1 lb 2 oz/500 g | peas |
| | olive oil for deep-frying |
| | salt and pepper |

**For the accompaniment (optional):**

potatoes
noodles
rice pilaf

**For the garnish:**

the whites of 2 leeks

When the first winter frosts set in, it is customary in the Basque Country to prepare veal cheeks in Rioja. Emilio González Soto gave some thought to this hearty satisfying dish, and decided to make a few changes.

The preparation of this recipe is easy, and yet the result is an absolute delight, thanks to the fine flavor of the tender veal cheeks. You can also make this dish with beef or pork, if you prefer.

Like all traditional dishes, this one also offers a wide range of different aromas. Depending on the size, the cheeks need to braise in the wine for 3 to 4 hours. Wine from the Rioja region goes particularly well with this dish, and that is what the chef uses. The controlled mark of origin is known all over Spain to represent quality and lifestyle. What's more, the landscape, with its vineyards and wine villages, is as unique as its excellent wines. Of course, you can also use any other red wine you happen to have to hand.

The mild chiles are an essential ingredient in Basque cuisine, and in this case they provide the spiciness for the sauce. The *pimientos choriceros* can be recognized by their long shape and dark red color. They are also ground and used to make the chorizo sausage.

To add a little more color to this traditional dish, the chef decided to use fresh peas. Ensure that the pods are a rich green and firm with no blemishes. Fresh pods will keep in the refrigerator for two or three days. Shelled peas do not need to be washed.

The leek makes the wine sauce wonderfully mild. The fried white part is used as garnish.

Trim the veal cheeks, then cut off the tendons and fat.

Heat ²/₃ cup (200 ml) olive oil in a pot, and fry the veal cheeks. Dissolve the veal stock in 4 tbsp (60 ml) water, and add to the pot. Peel the red onions. Wash the tomatoes and leeks.

Thinly slice the onions, tomatoes, and leeks, then put in the pot. Add the unpeeled garlic cloves and the whole chiles. Cover, then simmer gently for about 10 minutes, stirring occasionally. Season with salt and pepper.

# in Rioja

Pour over the red wine, and stir. Simmer gently for 3–4 hours, depending on the size of the cheeks. Shell the peas, boil in salted water for 6–8 minutes, and set aside.

Remove the veal cheeks, then strain the sauce through a sieve. Heat for 5 minutes, then add the cooked peas. To make the garnish, cut the white of the leeks into thin slices, and fry in olive oil. Set aside.

Cut the cheeks into evenly sized pieces, and arrange on plates. Pour over the sauce, and arrange with the deep-fried leeks.

# Partridge in

| | |
|---|---|
| Preparation time: | *50 minutes* |
| Cooking time: | *1 hour 40 minutes* |
| Difficulty: | ⋆ |

**Serves 4**

| | |
|---|---|
| 2 | partridges, each weighing 1 lb/450 g |
| 1 cup/250 ml | olive oil |
| 4 cloves | garlic, thinly sliced |
| 2¼ lb/1 kg | onions, finely chopped |
| 1 tbsp/15 ml | chicken stock concentrate |

| | |
|---|---|
| 2 | bay leaves |
| 1 sprig | thyme |
| 1 sprig | rosemary |
| 2 sprigs | parsley |
| 1 cup/250 ml | red port wine |
| 1 cup/250 ml | white wine (Albariño) |
| 1 cup/250 ml | sherry vinegar |
| 1 lb 2 oz/500 g | savoy cabbage |
| 7 oz/200 g | smoked ham |
| 4 | small potatoes |
| | salt |

The landscape of the Galician coast is marked by so-called rias—expansive, shallow estuaries a little like fjords. The inhabitants of the Atlantic coast in the north-west of Spain are passionate about their homeland, and they hold the customs of their ancestors—not least the culinary ones—in the highest esteem. Hunting is of particular importance to them, so it is hardly surprising that there are many dishes that include game. Partridge, which is greatly prized in Galicia, is a very precious quarry.

Here, María Lourdes Fernández-Estevez presents a recipe from her homeland. The spicy partridge in wine from the Rías Baixas region is particularly popular during the hunting season, in fall and winter.

Partridge has almost cult status on the Iberian Peninsula. In the Middle Ages, this little bird was reserved for princes and church dignitaries. In Spain, many children's fairy stories end with the phrase "they were happy and ate partridge," which is equivalent to "and they all lived happily ever after." Although partridge flesh is similar to that of chicken, it is served only on special occasions. Apart from young birds—no older than a year—the flesh of adult red or grey partridges is very firm and tasty. It is essential to observe the cooking times.

In this creation, the chef allows the wine to develop its full aroma. Albariño, which is renowned in Spain, is similar to a Riesling, which can also be used in its place.

Savoy cabbage, a typical winter vegetable, goes extremely well with partridge. Its firm bite and mild spiciness considerably enhance the dish. Make sure that your cabbage is firm with no tears or hard spots.

*Gut the partridge, and cut in half lengthwise. Clean, and rinse under running cold water. Truss each half—that is, tie the drumsticks and wings to the body. This way, the birds will turn an even brown when frying.*

*Heat ²/₃ cup (150 ml) olive oil in a large pot, and sauté the thinly sliced garlic and finely chopped onions for about 5 minutes.*

*Remove the garlic and onions, and blend in a blender. Put the partridge halves and the onion and garlic purée in the pot and fry, stirring continuously. Dissolve the chicken stock in ²/₃ cup (150 ml) hot water.*

# Albariño Wine

Add the bay leaf, thyme, rosemary, and parsley. Pour over the port, $^2/_3$ cup (150 ml) white wine, and sherry vinegar, then add the chicken stock. Cover, and simmer gently for about 1 hour and 30 minutes. Add a little salt.

Wash the cabbage and cut into strips. Finely dice the ham. Peel and deep-fry the potatoes.

Cook the cabbage in boiling water for 35 minutes. Drain. Heat the remainder of the oil in a casserole. Fry the cabbage and diced ham. Add the remainder of the white wine. Continue cooking for 3 minutes. Arrange the partridge on a serving dish. Serve with the cabbage and potatoes.

# Stuffed

| | |
|---|---|
| Preparation time: | *1 hour* |
| Cooking time: | *1 hour* |
| Difficulty: | ★★★ |

**Serves 6**

| | |
|---|---|
| 2 | carrots |
| 1 clove | garlic |
| 1 | onion |
| 1 | red bell pepper |
| 1 | green bell pepper |
| 3 | tomatoes |

| | |
|---|---|
| 4 | partridges |
| 4 oz/100 g | lean bacon |
| 4 oz/100 g | Serrano ham |
| 4 | anchovy filets in oil |
| 2 slices | white bread |
| 2 tbsp | flat-leaf parsley |
| 4–5 sprigs | thyme |
| 2 | bay leaves |
| 2 cups/500 ml | chicken stock |
| 1 cup/250 ml | dry sherry |
| | salt and pepper |

In the mountainous region of Málaga there is plenty of game. Accordingly, there are plenty of game dishes in the region—including this one by Javier Valero. The Spanish are enthusiastic hunters. The hunt is often more important to them than football and bullfighting. The most prevalent game varieties are quail, partridge, pigeon, pheasant, rabbits, and hares.

The mountains near Toledo are considered the "partridge region" of Spain. Huntsmen use decoys to lure the unassuming game bird: captive birds are used to lure their free-living cousins to the hunting grounds.

To make this dish a complete success, the chef recommends using a very young bird—ideally a red-legged partridge, as the flesh is particularly tender.

The birds are singed to remove all traces of feathers, then washed and patted dry. Gut them, reserving the liver for the stuffing. Loosen the ribcage with a small, sharp knife and remove all the small bones, trying not to damage the flesh. The recipe can also be made with quail, but you will need a lot of patience to bone these tiny birds.

The spicy stuffing can be further varied and enhanced by the addition of mushrooms, such as boulder mushrooms, chanterelles, or oyster mushrooms. To make it easier to grind the ingredients for the stuffing, it's a good idea to add a little olive oil.

Secure the stuffed partridges with toothpicks, or stitch them up decoratively with kitchen yarn and a trussing needle. Serve with colorful vegetables, sauce, and herbs.

*Peel the carrots, garlic, and onion. Halve the bell peppers, then remove the pith and seeds. Finely chop all the vegetables, and the tomatoes.*

*Gut the partridges and remove the legs, reserving the liver. Chop the bacon, ham and its fat, the livers, anchovies, and bread, and chop the parsley. Grind in the grinder. Season with salt and pepper.*

*Open out the partridges on a chopping board, and spoon the stuffing onto them.*

# Partridge

Fold the partridges together. Secure the cut edges with toothpicks.

Put the diced vegetables, thyme, and bay leaves in a casserole, then place the partridges on top.

Pour over the chicken stock and sherry. Cover the casserole, and bake in the oven (400 °F/200 °C) for 1 hour. Garnish the partridges with bay leaves and thyme. Serve very hot with the vegetables and sauce.

# Hen Pheasant

Preparation time: 35 minutes
Cooking time: 1 hour 15 minutes
Difficulty: ★

**Serves 4**

| 2 | hen pheasants, each weighing 1¾ lb/800 g |
| 4 | bay leaves |
| 1 | carrot, part cut into strips and part cut into round slices |
| 2 sprigs | fresh rosemary |

| 4 tsp/20 g | flour |
| 6½ tbsp/100 ml | olive oil |
| 1¾ oz/40 g | scallions (spring onions), halved lengthways |
| 1½ cups/300 ml | sherry vinegar |
| | salt and black peppercorns |

**For the garnish:**

bay leaves
fresh rosemary

Hen pheasant in *escabeche* (a marinade) is a specialty from La Mancha. In this area, which is extremely popular with huntsmen, game of all kinds features in countless guises.

This tasty dish is usually eaten cold. *Escabeche* used to be used to preserve and season foods, and it remains an essential part of Spanish cuisine today. Alberto Herráiz even believes that the success of this dish is determined by the quality of the oil and vinegar! The chef uses bay leaves to season the *escabeche*. This evergreen laurel thrives in the Mediterranean region. Its aromatic leaves are used in many braised dishes and casseroles, stuffings, and marinades.

This dish is easy to make and will keep well, because it is cooked in a preserving jar in a *bain-marie* (water bath). This means it can be enjoyed all year round, and not just during the hunting season. A *bain-marie* is used to cook certain dishes very gently, or to melt foods without the risk of burning.

Hen pheasants are greatly prized for the delicacy of their flesh. The bird, which is recognized by its gray-brown feathers, originally came from Asia, but became widespread throughout Europe in the Middle Ages. During the hunting season, from October to February, it is often available with its feathers still in place. If this is the case, ask the retailer to make the bird oven-ready for you.

Wild pheasant is quite literally a different kind of bird from the farmed variety, whose flesh is fattier and lacks the typical "gamey" flavor. The partridge, which is also highly prized in Castile, is an excellent substitute.

*Bone the hen pheasants and truss them, using kitchen yarn to bind the drumsticks and wings to the body. Slide a bay leaf, a little carrot, and rosemary under the yarn. Season with salt, and dust with flour.*

*Heat the olive oil in a casserole, and brown the birds carefully; remove.*

*Brown the halved scallions, peppercorns, carrot strips and slices, unpeeled garlic, and the bay leaves in the same oil for 3–4 minutes.*

# in Escabeche

Pour over the sherry vinegar and reduce. Add 1¼ cups (300 ml) water.

Put the pheasants back in the pot, and simmer gently for 35 minutes, turning occasionally.

Put the hen pheasants and accompaniments in a preserving jar, and cook in a bain-marie (water bath) for about 30 minutes. Slice the birds, and arrange on plates with the vegetables and sauce. Garnish with bay leaves and rosemary.

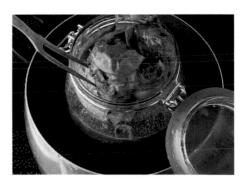

# Chicken

Preparation time:   1 hour
Cooking time:       1 hour 25 minutes
Difficulty:         ★★

**Serves 4**

| | |
|---|---|
| 1 | chicken weighing 3 lb 6 oz/1.5 kg |
| 1 cup/100 g | flour |
| ³/₄ cup/200 ml | olive oil |
| 30 | scampi |
| 2 | onions |
| 4 | ripe tomatoes, quartered salt and pepper |

**For the bouquet garni:**

| | |
|---|---|
| 2 sprigs | thyme |
| 1 sprig | rosemary |
| 2 | bay leaves |

**For the picada (spicy paste):**

| | |
|---|---|
| 2 cloves | garlic |
| 1 tbsp/15 g | skinned toasted almonds |
| 1 tbsp/15 g | skinned filberts |
| 2 tbsp/30 ml | red wine |
| 2 tbsp/30 ml | aniseed liquor |

Empordà, between Cap de Creus, Costa Brava, and Gerona, is famed for the excellence of its cuisine. Because of its proximity to the Mediterranean and the Canigou mountains, the chefs there invented numerous dishes on the subject of *mar i muntanya* ("sea and mountains"), combining fish and seafood with meat. Thus, for instance, there are meatballs with squid, and tuna with snails, to name but a few. Chicken with scampi is another wonderful delicacy in one of these unusual compositions.

To make sure the dish works well, Pep Masiques advises using a free-range chicken. The glass of water used for the sauce can easily be replaced by home-made stock: cover a piece of leek, a carrot, an onion, bay leaf, thyme, and parsley, plus the claws and heads of the scampi and the fish bones, with water. Cook until you have a strong stock.

When the chicken is cooked, strain the sauce through a sieve. Push any firm bits through the sieve with a pestle, because these bits contain plenty of flavor. Add a little water or stock to cook the ingredients added last.

In the Middle Ages, the cuisine of Catalonia chose a different course from that of Castile, and the preference for salty-sweet sauces such as *picada* dates back to that time. Combinations of dried fruit, garlic, parsley, and olive oil, or wine, are still enough to make any Catalan gourmet's pulse race today, and it is this combination that provides the right balance of flavors in this dish. The filberts are covered in boiling water, then drained and wrapped in a dish towel to make them easier to peel. Rub the nuts well until the brown skin flakes off. You can buy them ready-skinned, but skinned nuts soon turn dry, and even rancid.

*Divide the chicken into portions, and season with salt and pepper. Coat all the pieces in flour. Brown in very hot oil in a skillet for about 10 minutes. Place the chicken pieces in a casserole.*

*Spread the remainder of the flour over a large plate, and coat the scampi. Season with salt, and fry in the same skillet as the chicken portions. Put in a casserole and set aside.*

*Chop the onions, and braise for 20 minutes in the same skillet. Add the quartered tomatoes and the bouquet garni, and simmer. Sprinkle over 1 tbsp of flour, and continue cooking, stirring continuously. Add one glass of water and some salt, and simmer for 5 minutes.*

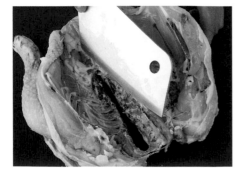

# with Scampi

Put the onion mixture in the casserole with the chicken portions. Simmer gently for 20–30 minutes. Remove the chicken, and strain the sauce through a sieve.

To make the picada, peel the garlic. Crush in a mortar with the almonds and filberts until you have a paste. Pour over the wine and aniseed liquor.

Place the chicken portions and the scampi in a casserole. Pour over the sauce, and add the picada. Cover with a lid, and heat through for 10 minutes. Arrange on plates, and serve.

# Paella

| | |
|---|---|
| Preparation time: | 15 minutes |
| Cooking time: | 30 minutes |
| Difficulty: | ★★ |

**Serves 4**

| | |
|---|---|
| 1³/₄ lb/700 g | rabbit |
| 4 | chicken quarters, ideally from free-range chickens |
| ²/₃ cup/150 ml | olive oil |
| 6 oz/150 g | sugar peas |
| 1 clove | garlic |

| | |
|---|---|
| 6 oz/150 g | runner beans |
| 8 | small artichokes |
| ²/₃ cup/150 ml | tomato sauce |
| ¹/₂ tsp | mild paprika |
| pinch | ground saffron |
| 2 cups/400 g | rice (ideally bomba) |
| 1 sprig | rosemary |
| ¹/₄ cup/50 g | pre-cooked white cannellini beans |
| ¹/₄ cup/60 g | shelled snails, cooked |

There are as many recipes for paella in Spain as there are towns and villages. The dish was named after the large pan in which it is cooked: the pan ensures an even distribution of heat, and has metal handles on either side. Originally, paella was a dish eaten by laborers in the region of Valencia, but soon it was enhanced by the addition of vegetables and snails, and rabbit and chicken on special occasions. In Spain, the men usually prepare the paella on a Sunday, so it is considered a holiday dish. Every village, every family, has its own recipe, using whatever they happen to have at the time: fish on the coast, meat and sausage inland, and vegetables, herbs, and spices.

The main and essential ingredient for paella is rice, ideally the round version called bomba, which absorbs lots of liquid without bursting. It is grown in some parts of Spain, such as Calasparra, where it also has a protected mark of origin. Bomba rice absorbs lots of liquid, yet remains *al dente* (firm), and nice and fluffy. It also absorbs the aromas from the paella pan. And therein lies the secret of a good paella. The best-known versions of this dish are paella Valenciana, in which the rice is cooked in a stock made of rockfish, and paella with squid and ink. In this recipe, Alberto Herráiz uses cannellini beans as well as meat, rice, and artichokes.

Paella cooked to all the rules is also served in Herráiz's restaurant, Fogón. Not only does Herráiz practice his craft, but he is also involved in the theory of cooking, and is a keen exponent of the retention of Spanish culinary traditions. He recommends serving a red Valdepeña from La Mancha with paella.

*Using a sharp knife, cut the rabbit and chicken quarters into small pieces.*

*Heat the olive oil in a paella pan, and brown the meat all over. Meanwhile, trim the sugar peas and cut them into pieces. Chop the garlic.*

*Put the runner beans and peas in the pan with the meat. Cut off the artichoke stalks and leaves. Cut the artichokes into quarters, and remove the "hay." Put in the pan and brown over a high heat. Add the garlic.*

Preheat the oven to 480 °F/250 °C. Add the tomato sauce to the meat and vegetables, then sprinkle over the paprika. Pour on 5 cups (1.5 l) water, and reduce by a third.

Add the saffron, and stir well.

Add the rice, and stir in evenly. Add the rosemary, cannellini beans, and snails. When the rice has absorbed the liquid, it will rise to the surface. Now cook the paella in the oven for a further 10 minutes.

# Desserts & Pastries

# La Mancha

Preparation time: 40 minutes
Cooking time: 40 minutes
Difficulty: ★★

**Serves 4**

| | |
|---|---|
| 1 tsp/5 g | butter |
| 1 | unwaxed lemon |
| 4 | eggs |
| ½ cup/100 g | sugar |
| ¼ cup/25 g | confectioner's sugar |
| 1⅓ cups/125 g | cake flour |

**For the sauce:**

| | |
|---|---|
| 1 | unwaxed lemon |
| 2 cups/500 ml | milk |
| ⅞ cup/200 g | sugar |
| 2 sticks | cinnamon |
| 1 | vanilla bean |

**For the garnish:**

| | |
|---|---|
| | ground cinnamon |

The Castilians are widely regarded as absolute gourmets. Every town, every village, in this delightful region in central Spain has its own sweet specialties. The recipe for La Mancha sponge cake is from Alcázar de San Juan.

These cakes are served, with milk to drink, for breakfast. Sponge is a very light and airy cake dough. Sieve the flour before mixing it, and brush the baking parchment with melted butter. Do not open the oven door while the cake is baking, otherwise the cake will collapse.

The lemon plays a special role in this dessert. This sun-drenched fruit is always associated with Spain, and is greatly prized for its high vitamin C content. If you want to use the peel, choose unwaxed specimens when shopping; otherwise wash them thoroughly in hot water.

The vanilla used in this recipe gives the milk an unmistakable aroma. The beans are the fruit of a climber from the orchid family, and first came to Spain with the Conquistadors. It is said that they first saw this spice when offered cocoa by the Aztecs. Impressed by the exceptional aroma of vanilla, they called it *vanillia* ("little bean"). Soon, the aromatic beans embarked on a triumphant march beyond the borders of the Iberian Peninsula, and conquered all of Europe.

Alberto Herráiz adds a cinnamon stick to the milk to counter the sweetness, as it provides a slightly tarter note. The rind of the cinnamon tree, it has a warm, mild sharpness. This tropical woody plant is grown primarily in Sri Lanka and China, and the plantations are scented by its penetrating, intoxicating scent.

*To make the sauce, first peel one of the lemons. Heat the milk, sugar, cinnamon, vanilla, and lemon peel in a pot. Simmer over a low heat for 40 minutes until reduced by a quarter. Reserve the cinnamon, vanilla, and peel as garnish. Leave the sauce to cool.*

*Line a baking sheet with baking parchment. Brush the parchment with melted butter. Grate the peel of the second lemon.*

*Separate the eggs. Whisk the egg yolks with a balloon whisk. Add the lemon peel and sugar, and combine well. Add the confectioner's sugar, and whisk until foamy.*

# Sponge Cake

Beat the egg whites until stiff in a second bowl with a clean balloon whisk.

Using a spatula, scoop the beaten egg whites onto the egg yolk mixture, and fold in. Add the flour and combine.

Spoon the dough into a forcing bag and, using a wide round nozzle, pipe strips onto the baking parchment. Bake (320 °F/160 °C) for about 10 minutes. Leave to cool. Put on plates, and pour over the sauce. Garnish with the lemon peel, cinnamon, vanilla bean, and ground cinnamon.

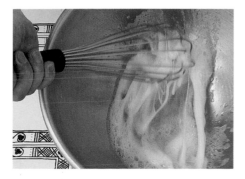

# Turrón

Preparation time: 50 minutes
Parfait freezing time: 3 hours
Chilling time
    crème anglaise: 30 minutes
Cooking time: 12 minutes
Difficulty: ★★

**Serves 4**

**For the turrón parfait:**

| | |
|---|---|
| 4 cups/1 l | cream |
| 9 | egg yolks |
| 1⅛ cups/250 g | sugar |
| 9 oz/250 g | turrón (Spanish nougat) |

**For the crème anglaise:**

| | |
|---|---|
| 2 cups/500 ml | milk |
| 1 | unwaxed lemon |
| 1 | vanilla bean |
| 4 | egg yolks |
| ⅜ cup/100 g | sugar |
| 1 tsp | cornstarch |
| 1 cup/250 ml | cream |

**For the garnish:**

| | |
|---|---|
| | mint leaves |
| 5 tsp/25 g | ground almonds |
| | red berries (optional) |

This exquisite dessert is typically Spanish. It is easy to make, and smells wonderfully of almonds and honey.

*Turrón*, probably Spain's most famous confectionery, is made in Jijona, about 12 miles (20 km) from Alicante on Spain's Mediterranean coast. The creamy, caramel-colored nougat is made during six months of the year only, because it is usually eaten at Christmas. The age-old recipe is yet another example of the country's Moorish heritage. The Moors ruled over Spain in the High and Late Middle Ages. It was they who introduced the Iberians to delicious sweets made of honey and almonds.

Almond trees have been growing in Alicante for about 12 centuries now, and the plantations stretch as far as the eye can see. The Marcona variety is used to make *turrón*, famous for its delicate, slightly bitter flavor and aroma.

The almonds are roasted whole, then ground and finally combined with orange blossom honey, egg whites, and confectioner's sugar to make the nougat. The extremely short cooking time takes place under the watchful eye of the *turronero* (the master confectioner), who is the only person able to take into account even apparently insignificant climatic changes on the day!

For this recipe, the egg yolks need to be heated with the sugar and *turrón* in a *bain-marie* (water bath) before the mixture is folded into the cream. This helps to prevent major changes in temperature, which would cause the cream to separate.

Cesar Marquiegui serves the parfait with crème anglaise. This delightful dessert is a great success at parties—and with children!

*To make the turrón parfait, pour the cream into a bowl and whisk with a balloon whisk until stiff.*

*Beat together the egg yolks and sugar until foamy, then stir in the crumbled turrón. Whisk in a bain-marie (water bath) for about 5 minutes until everything is combined. Then leave to cool, still stirring.*

*Pour the egg and nougat mixture into the cream, and fold in gently using a spatula.*

# Parfait

Pour the mixture into a tin lined with plastic wrap. Freeze for at least 3 hours.

To make the crème anglaise, bring the milk to the boil with the lemon peel and vanilla bean. Beat the egg yolks with the sugar and cornstarch. Strain the milk through a sieve onto the beaten egg yolks. Then leave to stand for 2–3 minutes.

Whip the cream until just holding its shape, then fold into the egg milk. Chill for 30 minutes. Arrange slices of the turrón parfait on plates, and surround them with a little crème anglaise. Garnish with ground almonds, mint leaves, and berries.

# Crema Catalana

Preparation time: 30 minutes
Chilling time: 2 hours
Cooking time: 25 minutes
Difficulty: ★

**Serves 4**

| | |
|---|---|
| 1 | unwaxed lemon |
| 4 cups/1 l | milk |
| ⁷/₈ cup/200 g | sugar |
| 1 stick | cinnamon |
| 1 | vanilla bean |
| 7 tsp/35 g | cornstarch |
| 8 | egg yolks |
| 2 cups/200 g | strawberries |

Many Catalonian families make *crema catalana* on March 19, which is St. Joseph's Day. Hens lay more eggs at this time of year than any other, so the large number required for this recipe are readily available. The tradition is so deeply rooted that, in Catalan, the dessert is called *crema de Sant Josep*.

Pep Masiques' choice is an authentic Catalonian dessert: the milk is flavored with cinnamon, vanilla, and lemon, and added hot to the egg cream. Then the crème is thickened slowly over a low heat until nice and smooth, and light yellow in color.

The combination of cornstarch and eggs thickens the crème. Rice flour used to be used for this purpose in Catalonia, but that took more time and was quite complicated.

Today, most Catalonians—and chefs in other regions—pour the crème into individual bowls, and sprinkle it with sugar when it is cool. The surface is caramelized with a hot iron, which does not take long because the sugar forms a very thin layer that soon melts and turns brown. However, Pep Masiques believes this makes the dessert far too sweet—and the caramel overpowers the delicate balance of aromas.

Chef serves the crème with fresh strawberries, whose fruity sweetness combines perfectly with the mild crème. The best Catalonian strawberries, or *maduixes*, come from the greenhouses of Maresme, the area to the north of Barcelona. Of course, wild strawberries—such as the ones found in the Pyrenees—are even better!

Peel the lemon. Pour 3 cups (750 ml) milk into a pot, then sprinkle over the sugar. Add the cinnamon, vanilla bean, and lemon peel, then bring to the boil. Lower the temperature, and leave the milk to steep.

Dissolve the cornstarch in 1 cup (250 ml) milk in a bowl. Beat together 8 egg yolks, and fold into the milk.

Strain the flavored milk through a sieve.

# with Strawberries

Pour the milk into a large pot and gently heat on the hob, gradually adding the egg yolk mixture, and stirring continuously.

Continue heating the milk, still stirring continuously, until it is thick and creamy. Remove from the heat, cool, and put in the refrigerator.

Wash and top the strawberries, and cut into quarters. Whisk the cooled cream again, then pour into a serving bowl. Garnish with the strawberries.

# Tetilla Cheese Crème

Preparation time: 40 minutes
Cooking time: 10 minutes
Difficulty: ★

**Serves 4**

**For the tetilla crème:**
½ cup/100 g sugar
2 cups/500 ml cream
1¼ cups/300 g tetilla cheese

**For the honey and orange waffles:**
1 stick/100 g butter
½ cup/100 g sugar
3 tbsp/100 g honey
1 cup/100 g flour
2 unwaxed oranges

**For the garnish:**
confectioner's sugar
honey

This crème, made of tetilla cheese and honey, was invented by María Lourdes Fernández-Estevez. She uses typical Galician ingredients for this delightful dessert.

Tetilla cheese is made mainly in the provinces of La Coruña and Lugo. It gets its name—it means "nipple"—from its curious shape. According to the chef, it dates back to the Inquisition, and was created by women in a determined effort to rebel against the strict rules of the time. The censors, disgusted at the representation of a bare breast in a church, apparently demanded its amputation. The women's answer was to invent a sensual, rich cheese in the shape of a perfectly formed bosom!

The Galicians love this mild, creamy cow's milk cheese very much. The light skin conceals a juicy, fine-tasting

mass. If you are not able to find it, you can use any other unpasteurized cow's milk cheese.

Always with an eye for the details, the chef chose to serve honey and elegant orange wafers with this dish. The delicate *tuiles* get their typical roof-tile shape if they are wrapped around a pasta roller to dry. If you are unable to obtain a silicone baking mat, you can use baking parchment, brushed with butter and dusted with flour, as a substitute.

In this recipe, the *tuiles* are flavored by the oranges. The best sort to use are Navel oranges, with their thick skin. Wash them thoroughly in hot water before grating them. Use shiny, heavy specimens. Oranges are quite hardy, and will keep at room temperature for several days.

*To make the waffles, melt the butter, add the sugar, and stir well with a wooden spoon until the sugar has dissolved.*

*Add the honey and fold in. Sieve the flour, then stir into the mixture. Whisk with a balloon whisk.*

*Grate the orange peel, stir into the mixture, and leave to cool a little.*

# with Honey

Place spoon-sized portions of the dough on a parchment-lined baking sheet, and bake (350 °F/180 °C) for about 5 minutes. Remove from the paper. Wrap around a pastry roller to shape if desired.

To make the crème, combine the sugar, cream, and tetilla cheese in a bowl. Transfer to the mixer bowl of the food processor.

Whisk in the food mixer until smooth and creamy. Arrange the cheese crème on plates, and garnish with a waffle. Serve with honey and confectioner's sugar.

# Mallorcan

| Preparation time: | 40 minutes |
| Standing time dough: | 10 minutes |
| Cooling time snails: | 24 hours |
| Rising time snails: | 3–4 hours |
| Cooking time: | 15 minutes |
| Difficulty: | ★★ |

**Serves 4**

| ⅓ cup/70 g | sugar |
| 1 | egg |
| 3 cups/300 g | flour |
| 4 tsp/20 g | fresh yeast |
| 9 tbsp/130 g | pork lard |
| | oil to grease worktop and baking sheet |

The Mallorcans are proud of these wonderful snails, which they call *ensaimadas*. Sometimes they are little appetizing squiggles, sometimes spirals the size of a wagon wheel. Visitors to Mallorca will be able to sample the vast array on offer—and take them home as edible souvenirs.

This delight is made with lard, which is spread onto the rolled-out pastry, and prevents the spirals from sticking together. Before ready-made yeast was available, people used a little fermented pastry as a rising agent.

The dough can sometimes be a little stiff if made in the food mixer, in which case a few drops of water will solve the problem. Some confectioners use milk instead of water. If the dough is too runny, add a little more flour.

Spread the lard carefully onto the dough with your fingers so it does not tear. When rolling out the triangles, make sure the dough stays in one piece. It is important to leave it to stand before rolling. Grease the triangles quickly and lightly using your fingertips, then roll them up like horns. It is easier if you brush a little oil on the worktop.

After chilling, the dough needs to rise for 3 or 4 hours. Check regularly to make sure it is not rising too much, but keeping its shape—especially if you are using fresh yeast and the room is warm.

The snails are popular at breakfast, served with hot chocolate or coffee. Gourmets like to enjoy their snails with honey, pumpkin jelly, cream, or even chocolate sauce.

*In the mixing bowl of the food mixer, combine the sugar with 6½ tbsp (100 ml) water, the egg, flour, and crumbled yeast. Knead with the kneading hook until the dough is smooth and sticking to the hook. Shape the dough into a ball, then leave to stand for 10 minutes.*

*Oil the worktop. Break the dough ball into pieces weighing about 2 oz (60 g) each. Knead them individually on the worktop, and shape them into balls again.*

*Using the pastry roller, roll each dough ball out into an oval. Beat the softened lard thoroughly in a bowl using a balloon whisk until it looks like meringue. Spread it over the dough, using your fingertips.*

# Snails

Using your hands, carefully shape each oval into a triangle.

Roll the triangles up, starting at the long side, so you have several thin dough rolls in front of you. Line the baking sheet with baking parchment.

Draw out the dough rolls and shape into snails. Cover with plastic wrap, and chill for 24 hours. Next day, leave the snails to rise at room temperature for 3–4 hours. Bake (350 °F/180 °C) for 15 minutes. Leave to cool, and dust with confectioner's sugar.

# Meringue Ice Cream

Preparation time: 1 hour
Standing time
  pastry: 30 minutes
Steeping time milk: 1 hour
Ice cream freezer: 20 minutes
Cooking time: 25 minutes
Difficulty: ★★

**Serves 4**

**For the orange tuiles:**
| 1⅓ cups/150 g | confectioner's sugar |
| 1/3 cup/35 g | flour |
| 5 tsp/25 g | ground almonds |
| 1 | unwaxed orange |
| ¼ stick/40 g | butter |

**For the meringue ice cream:**
| 1 cup/250 ml | milk |
| 1 | unwaxed lemon |
| 1 stick | cinnamon |
| ½ cup/100 g | sugar |
| 2 | egg whites |

**For the peaches:**
| 1 lb 14 oz/800 g | peaches |
| ½ cup/100 g | sugar |
| ⅛ stick | butter |

**For the garnish:**
| | ground cinnamon |

Refreshing, cinnamon-dusted meringue ice cream is a popular summertime treat on the café terraces of Valencia. Oscar Torrijos transforms *leche merengada* into a culinary experience by combining the ice cream with caramelized peaches and orange *tuiles*. The fruit and ice cream complement each other perfectly with the clever contrast of crispness and softness.

Starting with the basic idea, any seasonal fruit can be used for this recipe—plums, pears, or apples. The flavor of the peaches can be enhanced by adding a little vanilla sugar or pulp. Oscar Torrijos usually flavors them with *azucar tomillo limonero*, a specialty made of sugar and lemon thyme. We are using regular sugar. As soon as the fruit is covered in the butter caramel, Oscar Torrijos flambées it with Melocotón, a Spanish peach liqueur.

Because delicate, crispy cookies or cakes always go well with ice cream, the chef uses delicate, highly aromatic *tuiles* (brandy snaps) for this recipe, which require a little skill in the making. When they start to turn brown, they are taken out of the oven, carefully separated, and cut into precise circles with a cutter. They are then carefully removed from the baking sheet with a metal spatula, and quickly wrapped round a cylindrical kitchen appliance, such as a rolling pin or small bottle. They are then left to cool and harden.

The cultivation of oranges is important in the region of Valencia, and inspired Oscar Torrijos to flavor the pastry for the *tuiles* with the juice and grated peel of an orange. You can also use lemon peel, or ground cinnamon, instead.

To make the snaps, put the confectioner's sugar, flour, ground almonds, the juice and grated peel of an orange, and melted butter in a bowl. Combine until you have a smooth dough. Leave to stand for 30 minutes.

Line the baking sheet with baking parchment. Place small mounds of dough on the paper, and spread out until they are very thin. Bake (375°F/190 °C) for 5 minutes until light yellow. Then wrap around a rolling pin as described above.

To make the meringue ice cream, put the milk, lemon peel, cinnamon, and sugar in a pot, and bring to the boil. Remove from the heat, and leave to stand at room temperature for 1 hour. Strain the mixture through a sieve, and begin to process it in the ice cream maker.

# with Peaches

Whisk the egg whites until stiff. As soon as the ice cream starts to thicken, carefully fold in the egg whites and stir quickly. Continue to process it for a few minutes in the ice cream maker, then put in the freezer.

Skin and halve the peaches, and remove the stones. Cut each half into quarters.

Caramelize the sugar and butter. Add the peaches, and coat completely in the caramel. Using metal rings as molds, make circles of ice cream on plates. Then arrange the tuiles and peaches around the ice cream. Pour some of the caramel around the outside. Dust with ground cinnamon.

# Mantecadas

Preparation time: 30 minutes
Cooking time: 20 minutes
Difficulty: ✲

**Serves 4**

| ½ cup/125 g | sugar |
| 3 | eggs |
| 1 stick/120 g | butter |
| 1⅛ cups/130 g | flour |
| ½ tsp/2 g | baking powder |

**For the icing glaze:**

| 4½ cups/500 g | confectioner's sugar |
| 1 | egg white |

Which dessert lover could resist the appeal of these pretty little square cakes with the grainy sugar icing? *Mantecadas* were baked by a nun in the convent of Espíritu Santo of Astorga in the 19th century to an age-old recipe. In 1805, several confectioners in the town were making the sweet treat for their delighted customers. Around the 1850s, companies that specialized in making patisseries and chocolate looked at the recipe and finally began to market them. The cakes are still made and wrapped in their paper cases by hand today. Their fame has spread far beyond the borders of Astorga to the rest of Spain.

Santiago Pérez-García's is a relatively easy method, but the composition of the dough and the appearance of the little cakes are exactly in accordance with the old traditions. The name *mantecadas* comes from *manteca*, which refers both to the lard (*manteca de cerdo*) originally used in the recipe, and butter (*mantequilla*), which is used here. The flour is added to the egg-and-sugar mixture, and worked in with the hands. Reach down to the bottom of the bowl and push the dough up the sides, continuing in this fashion until it is smooth and homogeneous. The butter is worked in the same way.

Use a spoon or a forcing bag with a round nozzle to measure the dough into the paper cases. In the latter case, use a spatula to transfer the dough into the bag. Do not fill the cases to the top, as the cakes rise slightly while baking.

The sugar for the icing is mixed together with egg whites, and immediately spread out on a plate so it does not melt. It is then scattered over the cakes.

Put the sugar and eggs in the mixing bowl of the mixer, and blend at medium speed until the mixture leaves a trail.

Melt the butter in a bain-marie (water bath) or pot, and whisk until foamy.

Place a piece of baking parchment on the worktop. Combine the flour with the baking powder, and sieve onto the paper.

# from Astorga

Fold the paper down the middle, and pour the flour onto the egg mixture. Combine thoroughly.

Add the foamy butter, and knead until you have a smooth dough. Put spoonfuls of dough into small square paper cases.

To make the icing, pour the sugar into a bowl. Add the egg white, and rub the two together with your fingers. Sprinkle this mixture over the cakes and bake (430 °F/220 °C) for 20 minutes. Serve in the paper cases.

# Easter Week

Preparation time: 20 minutes
Cooking time: 15 minutes
Difficulty: ✳

**Serves 4**

| | |
|---|---|
| 2 cups/500 ml | milk |
| ²/₃ cup/150 g | sugar |
| 1 | vanilla bean |
| 8 slices | light bread with a thin crust |
| 3 | eggs |
| 2 cups/500 ml | sunflower oil |

**For the garnish:**

confectioner's sugar
ground cinnamon

The Spanish take to the streets in the days before Easter. The Easter Week processions are elaborate folk festivals, with repentants touring the streets in hooded garments, lavishly decorated carts with statues of the saints, and monks clad in habits. After this spectacle, families meet up for feasts of food special to Easter Week—*Semana Santa*—which differ from region to region. One is *torrijas*, not unlike fritters, which are served at the end of a delicious meal.

Use high-quality white bread with a dense crumb and thin crust, ideally a day or two old. Some countries call this dish "Poor Knights," because stale bread is, of course, something that poor people eat—in this case, as a delicious treat. You can also use toasting bread, but the end result will taste completely different.

José-Ignacio Herráiz scents the milk with a vanilla bean, but you can use a cinnamon stick, or grated orange, or lemon peel, if you prefer. The chef moistens each side of the bread with milk, making sure not too much is absorbed. In other variants of this dish the bread is soaked in honey, or even wine.

As soon as the bread is golden, it is sprinkled with cinnamon and sugar. The sugar melts on the hot surface, providing an intensive aroma. In La Mancha, our chef's home town, the milk-dipped bread is shaped into balls, dipped in egg, then deep-fried. It is served as a typical Easter Week dessert.

*Pour the milk into a pot, and add the sugar and vanilla bean. Bring to the boil, then leave to stand, and sieve.*

*Cut the bread into thick slices, and cut off the crusts so the slices are more or less square.*

*Place the bread on a plate, and ladle over a little of the vanilla milk. Turn the bread in the milk, so it is well soaked.*

# Fritters

Beat the eggs and pour onto a plate. Coat each slice of bread in the egg, then place on a second plate.

Heat the oil in a skillet, and fry the bread until golden, turning halfway.

Combine the sugar and cinnamon for the garnish on a plate. Coat the torrijas in it while they are still hot. Serve warm.

# Andalusian

Preparation time: 30 minutes
Cooking time: 30 minutes
Difficulty: ☆

**Serves 4**

| | |
|---|---|
| 2¼ cups/250 g | flour |
| ⅔ cup/150 g | lard or Crisco |
| ½ tsp/3 g | baking powder |
| ⅜ cup/90 g | sugar |
| ½ tsp/3 g | ground cinnamon |

When the Moors conquered Andalusia in the Middle Ages, they brought with them a number of recipes for delicious sweets and confectionery. Some of these recipes have survived in monasteries and convents over the centuries—including this one for *polvorones*, little cakes made of flour, lard, and sugar. The name comes from the fact they crumble into dust in your mouth when you eat them. In Spain, the specialty is a popular Christmas gift.

Santiago Pérez-García makes several different versions of *polvorones*; this one is the simplest. He sometimes includes chopped almonds or toasted grated coconut in his creations. In his most extravagant version, he replaces the confectioner's sugar with a nougat mixture consisting of 50 percent toasted almonds, sugar, soft *turrón de Jijona*, and a strong brandy—the popular aguardiente.

The flour is roasted, which makes the cakes light brown. It is spread thinly on a baking sheet, and baked in the oven, stirring it occasionally with a metal spatula to prevent it from burning. The advantage of this procedure is that the flour becomes very dry—as dry as dust, in fact. Because the recipe does not use eggs or water, the cakes keep very well. The roasted flour is left to cool, and sifted before using if necessary.

The dough is rolled out to the right thickness, and circles cut out. To remove the dough from the cutter, press on it gently with your finger. The offcuts are then re-kneaded, rolled out again, and more circles cut. To check when the cakes are done, press on them with your fingertip: they should be firm and not sticky.

*Spread the flour out on a baking sheet, and bake in the oven for about 10 minutes. Leave to cool, then shape into a mound on the worktop. Make a well in the middle. Put in it the sliced lard, baking powder, sugar, and cinnamon.*

*Knead well with your fingers until you have a light brown dough. Shape into a ball.*

*Roll out to a thickness of ½ in (1.2 cm).*

# Polvorones

Use a cutter of 1½ in (3.5 cm) diameter to cut out circles. Keep re-kneading and re-rolling the offcuts until you have used all the dough.

Line a baking sheet with baking parchment, and arrange the cakes on top. Bake (430 °F/220 °C) for about 15–20 minutes. Leave to cool.

Arrange the cakes close together on the baking parchment, and dust with sifted confectioner's sugar.

# Retorcidos

Preparation time: 30 minutes
Standing time
  dough: 30 minutes
Cooking time: 10 minutes
Difficulty: ★

**Serves 4**

7 tbsp/100 ml   olive oil
1               unwaxed lemon

1 tbsp/15 g     aniseeds
7 tbsp/100 ml   white wine
3 cups/350 g    flour
1 sachet        baking powder
                confectioner's sugar
                  for dusting
                oil for deep-frying

For Julio Reoyo's spiral-shaped creation, the pastry is wound around sugar cane sticks, and baked. *Retorcidos* means "wound around," which explains where the name comes from.

The dough is a mixture of flour and olive oil, among other ingredients, which is flavored with lemon peel and aniseed. Spain is one of the world's leading producers of olive oil, which has been made on the Iberian Peninsula since Roman times. Today, most olive groves are located in Andalucia, particularly in the provinces of Jaen and Córdoba.

The largest quantities of citrus fruits are grown around Valencia and Murcia. Lemons are not the only fruit to be cultivated there; you will also find oranges, clementines, grapefruit, kumquats, and limes. The Moors were the first to grow citrus fruits in southern Spain, implementing their brilliant irrigation systems consisting of channels and hydraulic pump systems.

To chill the lemon- and anise-flavored oil, put the pot in the sink and slowly add the white wine, flour, and baking powder in spoonfuls, stirring continuously. When the pastry has been rolled out and cut, the *retorcidos* need to be "rolled up." Very dry, unflavored sugar cane sticks are ideal for this purpose. If you are unable to obtain one, a thin rolling pin may also be used. Use the tip of a knife to remove the spirals after deep-frying.

Chef allows two *retorcidos* per person. The pastry is dusted with confectioner's sugar, and could be accompanied by a lemon-scented crème anglaise, or raspberry coulis. The Spanish also like it with *leche merengada*, refreshing meringue ice cream.

*Heat the olive oil in a skillet. Peel the lemon, and fry the lemon peel and aniseeds in the oil. As soon as the lemon peel becomes transparent, remove it from the oil and dispose of it. Remove the skillet from the hob, and leave the oil to cool down.*

*Pour the aniseed oil in a bowl and gradually add the white wine, 2½ cups flour, and baking powder. Stir until smooth, then shape into a ball and leave to stand for 30 minutes.*

*Dust the worktop with the remainder of the flour. Roll the pastry out.*

Cut the pastry into evenly sized strips about ¾ in (1.5 cm) wide.

Wrap each strip of pastry around a very dry piece of sugar cane.

Deep-fry the pastry-wrapped sugar cane sticks in very hot oil. Lift out as soon as the pastry is golden yellow, and carefully remove the retorcidos from the sugar cane. Place on paper towels to absorb excess oil, then dust with confectioner's sugar. Serve warm.

# Roscas

Preparation time:    1 hour
Cooking time:    40 minutes
Difficulty:    ☆

**Serves 4**

| | |
|---|---|
| ³/₄ cup/170 ml | sunflower or soy oil |
| 1½ cups/170 g | flour |
| 1 tsp/5 g | cornstarch |
| 3 | medium-sized eggs |

**For the glaze:**

| | |
|---|---|
| 1⅛ cups/250 g | sugar |
| 4 | egg whites |
| 1⅛ cup/125 g | confectioner's sugar |

These little cakes are loved by many Spaniards. The Castilian specialty is called *Roscas de Castilla* or *Roscas de Santa Clara*. There are countless variants of the age-old recipe; this is one of the most popular ones.

The basics behind the egg-rich pastry are simple: use equal weights of egg, oil, and flour. Santiago Pérez-Garcia likes to enhance the aroma of the little cakes with anise essence, aniseeds, or aniseed liquor. He sometimes adds a little sugar to the pastry, but then dispenses with the glaze. If you do not have a food mixer, you can easily make the dough with a balloon whisk.

The most difficult part of this recipe is the glaze. First the sugar is dissolved in the egg whites, and the mixture then whisked in the food mixer. The confectioner's sugar is sifted, added to the egg white, and mixed again until the sugar glaze is firm and homogeneous. It must not have the texture of meringue, as it would then slide off the cakes. If this happens, add a little water to the mixture, and stir until the mixture thins. If the glaze should be too runny, drain some off, then whisk again.

The *roscas* will dry very quickly when glazed on one side. Put the baking sheet in the preheated oven, and leave them to dry with the door open. After a few minutes, press a fingertip on one of the cakes to see if the top is firm. The glaze should form a firm, shiny coating. If this is not the case, then just return the cakes to the oven for a few more minutes.

*Combine the oil, flour, cornstarch, and eggs in the mixer bowl.*

*Beat until the dough is firm and thoroughly mixed.*

*Use a spatula to transfer the dough into a piping bag with a round nozzle.*

# de Castilla

Pipe small circles of dough onto a baking sheet, and bake (350 °F/180 °C) for 30 minutes.

To make the glaze, heat the sugar and the egg whites in a pot, stirring continuously, until the sugar has dissolved. Transfer to the mixer bowl. Add the fine confectioner's sugar, then beat until you have a thick, white sugar glaze.

Dip one side of the roscas in the glaze. Put the cakes on the baking sheet, glazed side up, and bake in the oven with the door open for 3 minutes. Leave to dry, then dip the other side in the glaze and dry the cakes again.

| Preparation time: | 20 minutes |
| Cooking time: | 20–25 minutes |
| Cooling time: | approx. 1 hour |
| Difficulty: | ★ |

**Serves 4**

| 7 tbsp/100 g | butter |
| 1⅓ cups/150 g | confectioner's sugar |
| 2 | eggs |
| 1½ cups/200 g | ground almonds |
| | butter and flour for the cake pan |

Since the 9th century, millions of pilgrims have traveled to Santiago de Compostela in Galicia from all over Europe to see the grave of James the Apostle. They still visit the town's confectioneries for refreshment in the form of *Tarta de Santiago*, an exceptionally appealing cake decorated with the sign of the cross. Nobody knows whether the recipe for this culinary delight was first provided by a sweet-toothed pilgrim, or the invention of a local confectioner, and then named after Spain's patron saint.

Santiago Pérez-García is an expert on Spain's confectionery. Here he presents a recipe that he has perfected over the years. Apparently the cake was originally made without butter, but it complements the oil in the almonds beautifully, and makes the cake wonderfully soft. It is first whisked until frothy; if the dough is a little too hard it can be lightened with a little egg white. If the dough is too soft, add a little confectioner's sugar. There are several different variants of this cake; some contain milk or cream. Some confectioners use cinnamon or lemon peel for added flavor.

The bottom and sides of the cake pan are brushed with melted butter and dusted with flour. The chef then chills the pan for a while. This makes the butter harden again, and helps the flour to stick to the pan without either combining with the dough. Shake the pan to remove excess flour after chilling.

A template is used for the decoration on the *Tarta de Santiago*. Place a St. James cross made of wood, metal, or cardboard on the middle of the cake. Then dust the top of the cake with a thin layer of confectioner's sugar, and remove the cross.

*Beat together the butter and ⅞ cup (100 g) confectioner's sugar in the bowl of the food mixer until the mixture turns yellow and thickens.*

*Add the eggs and continue beating until the mixture is creamy.*

*Fold in the ground almonds.*

# de Santiago

Brush a round cake pan with melted butter, and dust with flour. Chill the pan for a few minutes.

Pour the dough into the pan and bake in a preheated oven (350 °F/180 °C) for 20–25 minutes. Turn the cake out of the pan, and leave to cool.

Place the cake on a baking sheet. Put a St. James cross on the middle of the cake, and dust the surface with confectioner's sugar. Carefully remove the cross, leaving its impression on the cake.

# Fuengirola

Preparation time: 30 minutes
Ice cream freezer: 20 minutes
Cooking time: 30 minutes
Difficulty: ★★

**Serves 6**

**For the ice cream:**

| | |
|---|---|
| 10 | egg yolks |
| ⅞ cup/200 g | sugar |
| 1 | vanilla bean |
| ¼ cup/60 g | candied orange peel |
| 2 cups/500 ml | milk |
| ½ cup/125 ml | cream |

**For the cakes:**

| | |
|---|---|
| 1 | orange, with peel grated and juice reserved |
| 1⅛ cups/250 g | sugar |
| ⅜ cup/50 g | confectioner's sugar |
| 1 tsp/5 g | ground cinnamon |
| 6½ tbsp/100 g | candied orange peel |
| 1¾ sticks/200 g | butter |
| 3 | eggs |
| 2⅛ cups/250 g | flour |

**For the garnish:**

fresh mint leaves
candied orange peel

The bathing resort of Fuengirola is situated on the Costa del Sol, close to Málaga and Marbella. It is famed for the fine white sand of its beaches, its historic buildings, and almost tropical climate. Javier Valero invites you to sample the juicy orange cake and refreshing ice cream dessert named after this popular holiday destination.

The ice cream must be made first, since it can then chill in the freezer compartment until ready to serve. It is a classic vanilla ice cream based on *crème anglaise*. You can either scrape the pulp out of the vanilla bean and add it directly to the milk, or use ready-made vanilla extract. Adding tiny pieces of candied orange peel makes for a particularly delicious ice cream. Cinnamon is also an excellent spice. Once the *crème anglaise* has thickened, leave it to cool. Then continue making the ice cream in the ice cream maker.

To make the cakes, begin by whisking together the melted butter and sugar, then add the remainder of the ingredients. This makes the dough very homogeneous. You can also do this using a food processor or hand-held electric mixer.

Javier Valero has devised a very practical method for baking and turning out the little cakes. The dough is spooned into coated cake pans with smooth sides. Because it is quite soft, the cakes are easy to remove and look delicious. Professional confectioners use cake rings, which they simply place on top of a baking sheet lined with baking parchment.

The cakes are brushed with melted butter and dusted with confectioner's sugar before baking, which makes the top golden and crispy.

*To make the ice cream, put the egg yolks with the sugar, vanilla, and candied orange peel in a bowl. Combine well.*

*Bring the milk and cream to the boil in a pot, and immediately add to the egg mixture in portions. Heat on the hob for 10 minutes until thickened, stirring continuously. Leave to cool. Then put in the ice cream maker to finish the process. Finally, chill in the freezer compartment.*

*To make the cakes, grate the orange peel into a bowl for the cakes. Add the sugar, cinnamon, chopped candied orange peel, 1 stick softened butter, eggs, and orange juice. Beat well with an electric mixer.*

# Cakes

Gradually add the flour, stirring continuously, until you have a smooth dough.

Spoon the dough into little cake pans.

Melt the remainder of the butter. Brush over the tops of the cakes, and dust with confectioner's sugar. Bake (340 °F/170 °C) for 20 minutes. Cool. Place 1 scoop of ice cream on each cake. Surround with candied orange peel, and garnish with mint leaves.

# Tocinillos

Preparation time: 20 minutes
Cooking time: 30 minutes
Difficulty: ★

**Serves 4**

| 10 | egg yolks |
|----|-----------|
| 4 | eggs |
| ⁷⁄₈ cup/200 g | sugar |
| | glucose for the pans (optional) |

When the nuns in Madrid's convents used to treat themselves to something special on Sundays, they were presumably thinking of the heaven that awaited them at the end of their earthly lives. *Tocinillos de cielo*—"Heaven's little pigs"—is one of Spain's oldest and most popular desserts.

The recipe for this flan is not complicated. Whole eggs are blended with egg yolks and sugar syrup. Santiago Pérez-García has dozens of variants in his repertoire. Why not flavor it with orange or lemon juice? Or add a coating of chocolate, or a dusting of cocoa powder? Some chefs use milk instead of water for the syrup.

To make it easier to remove the flans from the molds, chef brushes them with warm glucose, but caramel is a good substitute. Savarin molds can be used for a different shape of the *tocinillos*.

When adding the syrup to the beaten eggs, stir continuously while doing so to combine the ingredients thoroughly. However, do not beat the mixture; it must not become frothy. The water must be bubbling before the molds are put in the steamer insert, because the mixture has to set as quickly as possible or the sugar will sink to the bottom—it is heavier than water and egg yolks.

Before he steams the flans, our chef places a tea towel between the pot and the lid. The cloth absorbs the rising steam, preventing water from dripping on the flans and causing unsightly holes.

For the garnish, a pattern of caramel or chocolate is drawn on the bottom of the serving plate, the *tocinillos* arranged on top. Garnish with mint.

*Put the egg yolks and the whole eggs in a bowl. Brush a little warmed glucose on the flan pans with your fingers. Bring some water to the boil in a steamer.*

*To make the syrup, put the sugar in a pot and add 7 tbsp (100 ml) water. Bring to the boil briefly, then remove instantly from the heat.*

*Beat the eggs. Add a little of the hot syrup, stirring continuously. Combine well, and strain through a sieve if necessary.*

# de Cielo

Use a small ladle to pour the crème into the prepared pans.

When the water in the steamer is simmering, place the custards in the insert. Cover with a lid and cook for 15–20 minutes. Remove from the pot and leave to cool.

Carefully shake the pans to remove the custards, and tip them onto a plate. Serve as soon as possible.

*Preparation time:* 1 hour
*Standing time*
*cream:* 40 minutes
*Cooking time:* 1 hour 5 minutes
*Difficulty:* ★★

**Serves 4**

**For the tostadas:**
| | |
|---|---|
| 6 cups/1.5 l | milk |
| ⅞ cup/200 g | sugar |
| ½ stick/50 g | butter |
| 3 sticks | cinnamon |
| 1 | unwaxed lemon |
| 7 | egg yolks |
| 1⅛ cups/125 g | cornstarch |

**For deep-frying:**
| | |
|---|---|
| 2 | eggs |
| | flour |

| | |
|---|---|
| | olive oil |
| 1 strip | unwaxed lemon peel |

**For the walnut sauce:**
| | |
|---|---|
| ½ cup/50 g | walnuts |
| 1 stick | cinnamon |
| 1 tsp | ground cinnamon |
| 1 cup/250 ml | milk |
| ¼ cup/45 g | sugar |

**For the garnish:**
| | |
|---|---|
| 4 tsp/20 g | sugar |
| 1 tsp | ground cinnamon |
| | walnut kernels |
| | cinnamon sticks |

*Tostadas de crema con intxaursalsa*, a milk dessert served with a walnut sauce, is popular at carnival time during February in the Basque Country—and especially loved by children.

This nutritious and original dessert is quite easy to make. It consists of milk, butter, egg yolks, sugar, and cornstarch, which are blended to a fairly thick cream and then coated in flour and deep-fried in olive oil.

The characteristic scent is cinnamon. The spice, which is popular in oriental cuisine as well as Spanish, has a strong, penetrating scent, and is prized for the warmth and piquancy of its aroma. The dried bark of the cinnamon tree is rolled into long tubes, which are cut into pieces before being offered for sale.

The lemon adds a special touch to this recipe. The fruit, which is very popular in Spain, is known for its high vitamin C content. Because the peel is used in this recipe, try to buy unwaxed fruits. If this is not possible, wash the fruits well in hot water before using.

The *tostadas* are served with a walnut sauce, *intxaursalsa* in Basque. The rich, slightly creamy sauce transforms this sweet into an elegant dessert.

Walnuts—originally from Asia—contain lots of copper and magnesium. The highly nutritious kernels are used whole, chopped, or ground. Once cracked, the nuts must be kept in an airtight container and protected against light, warmth, and moisture. They are used in many recipes for cakes, cookies, desserts, and pastries, and also as a garnish.

Crush the walnuts for the sauce in a mortar. Heat 1 cup (250 ml) water in a pot with both types of cinnamon, and add the crushed nuts. Boil until you have a smooth mixture. Remove the cinnamon stick, and reserve for garnishing.

Heat the milk and sugar in a pot. Add this liquid to the nut mixture in ladles. Simmer gently for 20 minutes, stirring frequently with a spatula.

To make the tostadas, bring 4 cups (1 l) milk to the boil with the sugar, butter, cinnamon stick, and lemon peel. Boil for 3 minutes, then remove the lemon peel and set the cinnamon stick aside.

# Walnut Sauce

Beat the egg yolks in a bowl with a balloon whisk. Add the remainder of the milk and the cornstarch, and stir well. Pour this mixture onto the hot milk. Cook for 5 minutes, stirring well.

Arrange the crème on a plate and leave for 30–40 minutes. Cut out round cookies with a cookie cutter, and coat in flour. Break 2 eggs into a bowl, and beat. Combine the sugar and cinnamon in a bowl.

Dip the tostadas in flour, then in beaten egg, and deep-fry in olive oil with a piece of lemon peel. Sprinkle over the cinnamon sugar, and arrange with the nut sauce. Serve garnished with walnut kernels and cinnamon sticks.

# Marzipan

Preparation time: 45 minutes
Standing time
   turrones: 2–3 days
Cooking time: 35 minutes
Difficulty: ★★

**Serves 4**

**For the egg turrón:**
3 egg yolks
3¼ cups/450 g ground almonds

**For the cream turrón:**
4 tsp/20 g powdered milk
6 tbsp/90 ml cream
3¼ cups/450 g ground almonds

**For the chocolate turrón:**
6 tbsp/90 ml cream
4 tsp/20 g cocoa powder
3¼ cups/450 g ground almonds

**For the invert sugar:**
2¼ cups/500 g sugar
1 lemon, juiced

**For the sugar syrup:**
¾ cup/170 g sugar

Valencia has been famous for its *turrón* for centuries. This is a moist nougat mixture made of almonds and sugar. In the 16th century, the town council of Alicante presented high-ranking visitors with the sweet delicacy to welcome them. Since then, itinerant sellers have taken this specialty far beyond the region's borders.

Santiago Pérez-García chose three versions of marzipan *turrones*: ground almonds are kneaded with sugar syrup and either eggs, cream, or chocolate. To make things a little easier, the invert sugar and syrup are made at the beginning of the process, then divided into three portions for use in each of the three variants.

Once you have incorporated whatever is required for your particular choice—eggs, cream and milk powder, or cream and cocoa—and the last two sugar products, the mixture is

heated on the hob until it thickens and starts to bubble. This is when the ground almonds are added. To check the consistency, put a little of the mixture on a spatula. It should be easy to spread out but still a little sticky. If it is too soft, add some ground almonds; if too hard, add a little more invert sugar.

The *turrón* has to be left in the mold for three days to make sure it has the right "bite." Level off the surface with your hand, then cover it with a piece of baking parchment you have cut to size. The whole mold is then covered with a further piece of paper that protrudes beyond the rims. Once ready, the *turrón* will keep well for two to three weeks.

To make sure the cut surfaces are smooth and even, our chef carefully rubs the blade with the inside of a lemon after every cut.

*For the invert sugar, put the sugar in a bowl, and add 6 tbsp (90 ml) of water and 4 tbsp (60 ml) of lemon juice. Bring to the boil, stirring continuously. For the sugar syrup, bring 4 tbsp (60 ml) of water and the sugar to the boil, and reduce. Set aside.*

*For the egg turrón, combine the egg yolks with a third of the invert sugar and a third of the syrup. Bring to the boil, stirring continuously. For the cream turrón, combine the milk powder with the cream, a third of the invert sugar, and a third of the syrup, then cook.*

*For the chocolate turrón, combine the remainder of the syrup with the cream, cocoa powder, and the final third of the invert sugar, and cook as before until the mixture has thickened and started to bubble.*

# Turrones

Add the ground almonds to each of the three mixtures, and fold in thoroughly with a spatula until the mixtures are absolutely smooth and homogeneous.

Place each mixture in a separate, high-sided rectangular pan. Smooth the surface, and place a piece of baking parchment on top. Leave for 2–3 days.

Turn out the turrón blocks onto a chopping board. Brown the egg turrón under the broiler for a few moments. Cut each block into evenly sized pieces, and arrange artistically on a plate.

# Yemas

Preparation time: 30 minutes
Chilling time: 1 day
Cooking time: 10 minutes
Difficulty: ★

**Serves 4**

1 ⅛ cups/250 g    sugar
15            egg yolks
1             lemon
            confectioner's sugar
            for the worktop

The Castilians have always had a penchant for desserts of all kinds. A 17th-century confectioner in Ávila, to the west of Madrid, first invented these little balls of baked dough that are dipped in sugar and caramelized. His son had the brilliant idea of naming the *yemas* after a famous local saint: Teresa of Ávila, the founder of the Order of Carmelites. The sweet-toothed saint was famous for saying: "God is everywhere—even in our cooking pots."

Today, the recipe for *yemas de Santa Teresa* is honored in a number of different versions. In this variation, the balls are coated in fine sugar and singed with a hot iron to become *yemas de Léon*. The standard Madrid version is coated in caramel.

The eggs, sugar, and lemon juice are whisked for a long time over a low heat. Santiago Pérez-García recommends that you scrape the bottom and sides of the pot frequently so that the ingredients all cook evenly. Towards the end of the cooking time the mixture looks like thick, yellow mayonnaise. It is then whisked again hard with a balloon whisk until it comes away from the sides of the pot, like choux pastry.

The chef adds a few drops of lemon juice to the mixture, but does not believe that any further aromas are required. If the cooled mixture is too soft to shape into balls, a little sugar can be added to make it firmer.

How the *yemas* are finished varies from region to region, and chef to chef. If you do not have an iron to brown them, you can caramelize them under the broiler, or grill. However, they look and taste equally good just dipped in confectioner's sugar or cocoa powder.

*Place the sugar in a pot, and add the egg yolks and a few drops of lemon juice. Whisk with a balloon whisk, and heat over a low heat until you have a fairly thick dough.*

*Using a spatula, spread the mixture over a high rectangular tin and smooth off. Cover with plastic wrap, and chill for one day.*

*Next day, dust the worktop with confectioner's sugar, and knead the dough with your fingers. Shape into a ball.*

# de Léon

Using your hands, roll the dough out into an evenly shaped roll.

Cut the roll into pieces, shape each piece into a plum-sized ball, and coat all over in the remainder of the confectioner's sugar.

Place the yemas on a baking sheet, and briefly singe the top of each ball with the red-hot iron to caramelize. You can also do this under the broiler.

# The Chefs

**María Lourdes Fernández-Estevez**

**Emilio González Soto**

**Alberto Herráiz**

**José-Ignacio Herráiz**

**Rufino Manjarrès**

**Cesar Marquiegui**

**Pep Masiques**

**Santiago Pérez-García**

**Julio Reoyo**

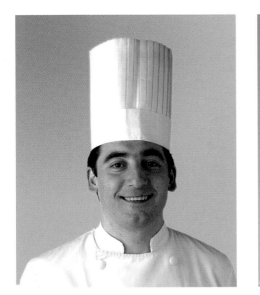

**José Luis Tarín Fernández**

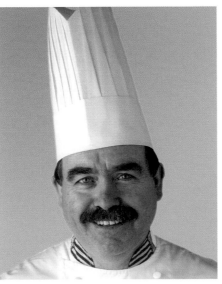

**Oscar Torrijos**

**Javier Valero**

**Abbreviations:**

1 oz = 1 ounce = 28 grams
1 lb = 1 pound = 16 ounces
1 cup = 8 ounces *(see below)
1 cup = 8 fluid ounces = 250 ml (liquids)
2 cups = 1 pint (liquids)
1 glass = 4–6 fluid ounces = 125–150 ml (liquids)
1 tbsp = 1 level tablespoon = 15–20 g *(see below) = 15 ml (liquids)
1 tsp = 1 level teaspoon = 3–5 g *(see below) = 5 ml (liquids)

1 kg = 1 kilogram = 1000 grams
1 g = 1 gram = $1/1000$ kilogram
1 l = 1 liter = 1000 milliliters = approx. 34 fluid ounces
1 ml = 1 milliliter = $1/1000$ liter

*The weight of dry ingredients varies significantly depending on the density
factor, e.g. 1 cup flour weighs less than 1 cup butter.
Quantities in ingredients have been rounded up or down for convenience,
where appropriate. Metric conversions may therefore not correspond exactly.
It is important to use either American or metric measurements within a recipe.

© for the original edition: Fabien Bellahsen and Daniel Rouche

Design and production: Fabien Bellahsen, Daniel Rouche
Photographs and technical direction: Didier Bizos
Photographic assistant: Gersende Petit-Jouvet, Morgane Favennec, Hasni Alamat
Editors: Élodie Bonnet, Nathalie Talhouas
Assistant Editor: Fabienne Ripon
Coordination: Alberto Harráiz

Original title: *Délices d'Espagne*

ISBN of the original edition: 2-84308-356-7
ISBN of the German edition: 3-8331-2439-3

© 2006 for the English edition:
Tandem Verlag GmbH
KÖNEMANN is a trademark and imprint of Tandem Verlag GmbH

Translation from German:
Mo Croasdale for Cambridge Publishing Management Limited
Edited by Sandra Stafford for Cambridge Publishing Management Limited
Proofread by Jan McCann for Cambridge Publishing Management Limited
Typeset and managed by Cambridge Publishing Management Limited

Project Coordinator: Isabel Weiler

Printed in Germany

ISBN 3-8331-2035-5

10 9 8 7 6 5 4 3 2 1
X IX VIII VII VI V IV III II I